What wakes you up at nigl
your job situation? Anxiety
of one of your children? If
you're not alone—but you don't need to stay stuck there.

I've read Chris's devotions for years, and he regularly speaks truth into my life. Now, in his typically insightful and thoughtful manner, Chris Tiegreen invites you to journey with him as he considers what it means to allow God to carry our loads. While your burdens may still be there when you finish this book, I suspect they will suddenly seem a lot lighter.

Ron Blue
President, Kingdom Advisors

Masterful, calming and wise. A liberating study on what it means not to battle burdens but to let God carry them. A great gift for anyone eager to exchange spiritual struggles for victorious freedom. Probing and life-changing. Makes me want to say "aaaaah!"

Patricia Raybon
Author, *I Told the Mountain to Move*

Don't read this book! At least not if you like simple formulas, clichés, and easy answers, because Chris's thoughtful treatment of this challenging topic will just frustrate you. If, however, you're tired of carrying burdens God never intended you to bear, let Chris serve as a trusted guide to help you lighten your load and surrender the delusion that you'll someday get it all under control if you just try a little harder.

Phil Tuttle
President, Walk Thru the Bible

Tricia —

You have been on my mind and in my prayers. My daughter struggles with anxiety & I gave this book to her (accidentally!) and she found it very helpful.

Praying that God will help you find the way out of where your mind wants to go. He is the healer of bodies _and_ minds.

Trust God & be blessed —
Suzy Edwards

Anxiety does not empty tomorrow of its sorrows, but only empties today of its strength.
Charles Spurgeon

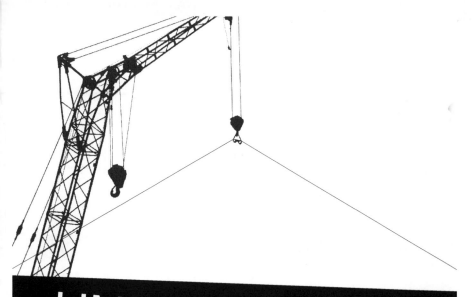

UNBURDENED

the secret to letting God carry the things that weigh you down

chris tiegreen

TYNDALE
MOMENTUM™

The nonfiction imprint of
Tyndale House Publishers, Inc.

Visit Tyndale online at www.tyndale.com.

Visit Tyndale Momentum online at www.tyndalemomentum.com.

TYNDALE, Tyndale Momentum, and Tyndale's quill logo are registered trademarks of Tyndale House Publishers, Inc. The Tyndale Momentum logo is a trademark of Tyndale House Publishers, Inc. Tyndale Momentum is the nonfiction imprint of Tyndale House Publishers, Inc., Carol Stream, Illinois.

Unburdened: The Secret to Letting God Carry the Things That Weigh You Down

Designed by Mark Anthony Lane II

Published in association with the literary agency of Mark Sweeney & Associates.

Unless otherwise indicated, all Scripture quotations are taken from the *Holy Bible,* New Living Translation, second edition, copyright © 1996, 2004, 2007 by Tyndale House Foundation. (Some quotations may be from the NLT, first edition, copyright © 1996.) Used by permission of Tyndale House Publishers, Inc., Carol Stream, Illinois 60188. All rights reserved.

Scripture quotations marked NIV are taken from the Holy Bible, *New International Version,*® *NIV.*® Copyright © 1973, 1978, 1984 by Biblica, Inc.® Used by permission. All rights reserved worldwide.

Scripture quotations marked NKJV are taken from the New King James Version,® copyright © 1982 by Thomas Nelson, Inc. Used by permission. All rights reserved.

For information about special discounts for bulk purchases, please contact Tyndale House Publishers at csresponse@tyndale.com or call 800-323-9400.

Library of Congress Cataloging-in-Publication Data

Tiegreen, Chris.
  Unburdened : the secret to letting God carry the things that weigh you down / Chris Tiegreen.
    p. cm.
  Includes bibliographical references (p.   ).
  ISBN 978-1-4143-2173-8 (sc)
  1. Christian life. 2. Liberty—Religious aspects—Christianity. I. Title.
  BV4509.5.T53 2010
  248.8´6—dc22   2010004054

Printed in the United States of America

Contents

Introduction

THE MOOD OVER Jerusalem was tense. The Jesus sect was inviting uncircumcised Gentiles into their allegedly "Jewish" gatherings, and Jerusalem's religious leaders weren't happy about it. So King Herod, always interested in appearing as Hebrew as possible—it helped compensate for his mixed heritage and his obvious Roman sympathies—took advantage of the opportunity. He arrested James the son of Zebedee and had him killed. The Jewish leaders were pleased.

They were so pleased, in fact, that Herod decided to take it a step further. He arrested Peter, an even higher-profile leader of the Jesus sect. Jews from across the empire were in Jerusalem for the Passover feast, and a public trial of a key figure in this controversial movement could turn into a huge political asset. Peter would be executed right after the feast while the city was still crowded with visitors. The sect would be shamed, its adherents would learn a valuable lesson about the dangers of unsettling a holy city, and Herod would be praised for taking decisive action.

Christians gathered in the home of Mary, mother of John Mark, and prayed their hearts out—with the kind of intensity and passion Jesus prayed with in Gethsemane, according to the language of the text.[1] They were desperate. Their leaders were being targeted, and their faith was rapidly dropping in the public's esteem. If Peter was killed, who would be next? These were frightening times.

Meanwhile, Peter was being guarded closely. He had escaped from prison years earlier, and Herod made sure he wouldn't escape again. This unarmed spiritual leader was guarded by four squads of four soldiers each who rotated six-hour shifts. Peter's wrists were constantly chained to a guard on each side of him while two other guards stood at the door. It would have been virtually impossible to find a physically comfortable position, and even more unlikely to be mentally or emotionally at peace. For all he knew, his days on earth were numbered.

Finally the Passover feast drew to a close. The night before Peter's trial—and probably his execution, too—the believers in Mary's house were praying as intensely as ever. God heard their prayers and sent an angel to the cell where Peter lay chained between two guards, sleeping. Not worrying about his trial, not replaying his defense over and over again in his mind, not wondering how the church would survive without him, but sleeping. In chains. On a stone floor.

A bright light shone in the room when the angel appeared. Still, Peter slept. The angel had to strike him on his side to get him to wake up. Even then, Peter thought he might be seeing a vision. Not until he was led out into the street and the angel left did he come to his senses. He went to Mary's house, where his friends seemed completely shocked that their desperate prayers had been answered. In spite of their fears, God demonstrated his ability to handle a crisis.

I've tried to imagine how I would feel the night before my impending trial and execution, and somehow I can't envision sleep entering the picture. I would be thinking obsessively about what I needed to say the next day, how I would respond to each and every possible twist in the trial, how my family and friends would handle the trauma, how they would get by without me, and what it's really like the moment you die. The weight of the situation would be heavy enough to emotionally paralyze me and to give me stomach cramps and heart palpitations. I would pray for a miracle almost constantly, pouring out my heart to God and explaining all the reasons it would make sense for him to deliver me. I would try to plan my last words to those I love and figure out how to get the messages to them. The one thing I would not do is sleep.

Somehow, Peter slept. He wasn't worried about his trial or its outcome. He was well acquainted with God's ability to rescue a prisoner, but he also knew that God had very recently decided not to rescue James. Still, he rested. He was at peace.

That would not have been possible if Peter was focused on his own agenda, concerned for his rights, worried about his future, or stressed about all the people who looked to him for leadership. Somehow he was able to put those concerns aside and trust God to do whatever God wanted to do. Peter faced one of life's most challenging, burdensome moments with a heart that was completely unburdened.

I would love to have the ability to do that. I've thought a lot about what it would take to approach life with that sense of freedom, and I think I've made progress in some areas. But like all of us, certain issues and events have an uncanny ability to push my buttons or get me wrapped up in my own concerns and anxieties. I can be remarkably unburdened about some things and alarmingly stressed about others. But a lifestyle of consistently being unencumbered by weighty matters eludes me more often than I would like.

> **Living in freedom from unnecessary strain is a universal craving.**

Even so, I felt an irresistible urge to write this book. The idea fascinates me. Is it really possible to go through all of the ups and downs of life and deal with all of its responsibilities and challenges with a sense of freedom? Is it realistic to think we can live weightlessly without detaching from the world or rejecting responsibility? Can we live real lives with real families and jobs and still not get loaded down with stress over our obligations? I think we can. Living in freedom from unnecessary strain is a universal craving. I think God gives us biblical examples of how to do it. I believe he designed us for just such a life.

The Unburdened Life

I figured I would write this book at a mountain retreat or in a beach condo—no distractions, nothing else on the calendar, no monumental to-do list hanging over my head. After all, it seems like writing about the unburdened life should best be done while having no burdens, right? Sadly, God didn't cooperate with my agenda. For some reason, he thought it would be best for me to write this book while life was screaming at me to be stressed out: while to-do lists grew out of control and deadlines shouted relentlessly and relationships needed serious attention and major life decisions hovered over my head and the economy was diving downward and people all around me were getting laid off and . . . well, you get the picture. Apparently, God doesn't think a discussion on "the unburdened life" is for people who are cruising. It's for people who are weighed down and about to buckle.

In a strange sort of way, that's good news. God always comes to us in our need. He doesn't show himself as our Deliverer when we're free or as our Healer when we're well. Our ability to see his love and his gracious attributes kicks in only when we're contending with the contradictions to them. His promise to deal with our worries isn't very precious to us when we don't have any. If there's ever a time to write or read or talk about the unburdened life, it's when the burdens are overwhelming.

We find ourselves in that condition more often than we'd like to admit. I've recently taken a silent inventory of responses when I ask people how they are doing, and they fall into two categories: "I'm way too busy" and "I desperately need more work." People in the first group are stressed by their workload, and people in the second are stressed by mounting financial debt. But hardly anyone says, "Life is great! I've got just the right amount of things to do, and it's all going well." The people of God have fallen in line with the rest of Western society and become a kingdom of jugglers. We've got issues—plenty of them—and while our theology tells us God will take care of us, our practical behaviors and attitudes don't exactly model that truth.

Think about that. What "good news" are we demonstrating for the world to see? Most of us go through seasons during which we're as stressed out as anyone. We have hope for the distant future—our eternity, for example—but the distant future isn't very compelling to people who are struggling to get by right now. Joy is supposed to be one of the distinguishing characteristics of the gospel, but I wonder how many Christians actually live in that reality. We who are allegedly empowered by the life of Another often seem strangely powerless to overcome the winds and waves of life.

Though twenty-first-century society intensifies our stress, carrying burdens is not a new phenomenon. Jesus told his followers not to worry about their lives and to bring their burdens to him—presumably because the human tendency even then was to worry and carry extra weight. In fact, I'm convinced that the fiasco in Eden long ago cut us off from a relationship of trust in God, and we've carried stress and anxiety ever since. We'll dig into that a little more later, but this is why faith and trust are such prominent themes in Scripture. The Psalms are full of exhortations to trust in God because it isn't our natural tendency to do so. Throughout history, people have sought remedies ranging from Hindu meditation to psychiatric medication. Burdensome issues are universal.

So is the desire to live with a light heart, and virtually every religion attempts to tell us how to do that. The normal Christian approaches to the unburdened life rightly center on trust and faith in God. That's what Jesus taught, and that's perfectly in line with the rest of Scripture too. Human beings, Christians included, have a fundamental trust problem—an endless capacity to second-guess what God has clearly spoken and to ask "what if?" about virtually every possible variable in our future. If you're like me, you can read a thousand promises from the very Bible we call

> **The Psalms are full of exhortations to trust in God because it isn't our natural tendency to do so.**

"infallible" and "inerrant" and still ask, "Lord, is that what you really mean?"

Christian thinkers and writers focus on this trust issue, albeit from different angles. Approaches that have helped me over the years include François Fénelon's *Let Go*; the "exchanged life" principle of *Hudson Taylor's Spiritual Secret* and other figures of faith from his era; and Andrew Murray's *Absolute Surrender*. All had major responsibilities and accomplished great things, but they learned to handle their burdens without undue urgency and strain. Their writings aren't always directly aimed at issues of stress and worry, but in focusing on the heart of the matter—surrendering self-will and dying to self—they cut away at the root of our problem. Though I think there's more to the issue than that, I've learned from their perspectives.

I've often wondered what would happen if we followed their counsel and simply let go of our concerns. Would the world fall apart? Would situations worsen because we aren't stressed about them anymore? Would all our dreams and desires fall into God's trash pile if we were no longer pestering him about them? Why don't we just "let go"? I don't know. We would certainly lose a sense of control, but maybe that's the point. Perhaps that's our fundamental problem— our false sense of control. It's an illusion, and it wreaks havoc on our sense of peace. But we desperately try to maintain it anyway. Why? Because we have a hard time trusting God.

That has certainly been true in my experience. I've been accused of being a little "intense." I'm driven by certain goals and desires—and probably quite a few past wounds—and have a really hard time letting up or relaxing for very long. I feel the weight of life's burdens more deeply than a lot of people I know. I have a few friends who are laid-back and relatively carefree, and I envy them. They would probably look at me in astonishment and say, "You're writing a book about being unburdened? Really? Umm . . . are you sure you're the right guy for that?" And they wouldn't be asking anything I haven't already asked myself. In a lot of ways, as I mentioned, I'm the least qualified person to write on this subject.

One of my pastors asked me what my next book was going to be about. I was embarrassed to even speak the title of this one, but I managed to mumble it—adding the part about how I'm the wrong guy to write it. "I think you're exactly the right person to write that book," this pastor said. "Only someone who has had to carry a lot could say anything meaningful on that topic."

There's a lot of truth in that perspective. I mean, do you really want to hear from one of those rare people who never seem to have a care—who have a naturally laid-back approach to life? Most of us aren't given the gift of a mellow nature, and we can't relate to those who are. The reasons I'm qualified to write about this are the exact same reasons I would think I'm not. I've fought epic battles in this area, and I know some strategies that work. I'm a guy with broken dreams scattered throughout my past, a long history of depression in my lineage, a fair share of struggles against family dysfunction, a brain-injured son, off-and-on financial pressures, a deadline-driven job, and an inability to say no until I'm hopelessly trapped under a heavy workload. I've stared into the piercing eyes of anxiety and fear. I've borne burdens that nearly crushed me to death. Like many people, I've suffered enormously from my own mistakes and the mistakes of others, and I've come up standing, sometimes even flying. I know many sides of this issue.

I know there are many well-intentioned Christians who give superficial advice on this topic, but I have no illusion that this is a superficial process. This book isn't a don't-worry-be-happy, God-is-in-control pep talk. You'll probably find the bumper-sticker message to "let go and let God" somewhere in these pages, but never in such blithe terms. The human psyche is a lot more complex than that, and God's solution for us goes a lot deeper.

Years ago, someone who had never met me before and had no information about my past or present circumstances felt led by the Spirit to give me a message. "I see you as a freight train," she said. "You're made of steel, and though you've taken a while to build up speed, God has given you the ability to pull a ton of weight." And I just kind of filed that message away. It rang true—I felt like I was pulling a ton of weight at the time—but there wasn't any instruction or guidance in it. I didn't know what to do with that picture.

But now that I've thought about it, I realize what it means. A freight train isn't unburdened when it starts rolling, straining so much that you can hardly imagine it pushing through a moderate breeze. But once it gets going, it looks and feels effortless. It just cruises through the countryside as if the journey is more valuable than the destination.

That's true of our burdened lives too. We struggle under the weight sometimes, but once we're rolling down the tracks, it doesn't matter how much freight we're pulling. In fact, the freight can work to our advantage, pushing us forward with its momentum. We may have trouble stopping, but we don't have to worry about holding up our cargo. It just comes along for the ride.

So now when I think about the unburdened life, I realize it's less about getting rid of our baggage than it is about carrying our loads with ease. It's true that we cast our burdens on the

> **The unburdened life is less about getting rid of our baggage than about carrying our loads with ease.**

Lord, but think about where they actually go: on the Lord who lives within us. The issues of our lives don't normally disappear when we cast our burdens on him. They simply get a lot lighter. The Spirit within us carries them as easily and breezily as a charging locomotive cruises through the countryside.

That's what this book is about. It won't teach you how to avoid responsibility or insulate yourself against serious issues by becoming detached and uncaring. Neither is it about how to escape and go live on a beach—at least not physically, though I've found that having a couple of palm trees in my spirit never hurts. It's about taking the burdens you currently carry and making them much, much lighter. It's about transferring the weight of your responsibilities from the weak shoulders of your flesh to the strong fingertips of God. It's about living in deep-down, heart-level freedom.

This book won't come across as a "how-to" manual. I've already declared how unqualified I am to approach the subject that way. No, this is more like a series of personal reflections on what it's like to struggle with heavy baggage and, more important, what it's like to release the weight of that baggage to someone much more capable of handling it. These words express the deep wrestling of a lifetime. And as I've freely admitted, this isn't an issue I've mastered. It's an ongoing process. But it's a process that most of us need to learn to share with each other. What follows is my attempt to do just that—to share where I've been. I hope you'll read it simply as one freight train telling other freight trains about the track he's been traveling.

CHAPTER I

FREEDOM

I REMEMBER THE feeling clearly. I had just completed a very difficult term and was driving home from college with an entire summer ahead of me. There were no more oppressive exams or papers hanging over my head, no messy relationship issues lingering in the background, no financial pressures in the foreseeable future, no nagging health problems. The windows were rolled down, and the fresh air of early summer washed over me at highway speed. Life felt good.

In a way, it's sad that I can remember that particular moment so many years ago. I wish it was one of many such moments, but it was unique—a brief haven in time, a last vestige of childhood—and I haven't felt that way since. That's why it sticks out in my memory. It was a very rare exception to normal life.

I want that feeling back. I didn't have it very often in childhood, and I certainly haven't had it since that summer break in college. But it seems to me that this is how we were designed to live—with hearts that aren't stressed out by the burdens of life but are free to soar and enjoy and dream. We feel alive when we aren't weighed down by burdens, and we instinctively know something's wrong when we are. It seems that we have an inherent desire to go through life weightlessly.

You know that desire. I know you do; everyone does. You get a glimpse of it every time you look forward to Friday or plan that desperately needed getaway. Whenever you get a brief respite, you kick back and enjoy the quietness and wish life were always so hassle free. Every desire to unwind, to take a break, to carve out some quiet time from a busy schedule, to escape into a book or movie, to dream about the day you retire, to laugh and forget about the demands on your life for a moment—it's all a hint of that craving to be as free as God intended for you to be. You want—we all want—to live without feeling like we're under extreme pressure.

We have an inherent desire to go through life weightlessly.

I can hear the objections already. "That isn't realistic." "God didn't intend for us to live without responsibilities." "You're describing childhood, not adulthood." And that's all true—to a degree, which we'll discuss later. But the Bible undeniably offers us a certain weightlessness to life, and most Christians aren't living in it. Though life in a broken world is full of concerns and problems, the "Good News" is supposed to actually be good. There are answers. There's a better way to live. Through God's promises and the hope and faith he stirs up within us, we can have a level of freedom that people who don't know him can't have. We don't have to submit to the oppression of our concerns. We are called "overcomers" and "more than conquerors" for a reason. No matter how heavy the weights on our shoulders are, we can't ultimately be defeated by them. The rest of the world can't say that. We have resources others don't have.

Don't Worry

For the most part, the crowds who were gathered around Jesus weren't very wealthy. They were people who got by on the basic necessities and who depended on seasonal rains for survival. They worked a full six days a week, generally from sunrise to sundown. They farmed, fished, worked with their hands in fabrics, metals, and woods, maintained simple homes, and trained and cared for their children. It was a simple life but not an easy one. Their welfare depended not only on weather patterns, but on compliance with Rome and the impulses of tax collectors. Their entire well-being could suddenly be threatened by an unexpected disease or a common thief. Many of their children didn't survive childhood.

They were familiar with hard economic and political realities and the fragile nature of life.

Like all of us, Jesus' listeners tended to preoccupy themselves with surviving and earning a decent living. They looked forward to God's Kingdom, but they spent most of their waking hours thinking about immediate needs. So what did Jesus tell this group of subsistence-minded people? "I tell you not to worry about everyday life—whether you have enough food and drink, or enough clothes to wear."[1] Why? Because that isn't what life is about. All they had to do was look at the birds of the air and the flowers in the field. God is in the business of taking care of little, insignificant creatures. How much more will he take care of human beings, the pinnacle of creation on earth? If he has invested his attention in the relatively small matters, won't he be much more committed to us?

These are such familiar verses that we often lose the impact of them. Try to read Jesus' words as though you are seeing them for the first time. Hear what he is saying. He isn't giving this crowd of people a slap on the back and telling them to eat, drink, and be merry today because they'll die soon enough anyway. He isn't telling them that they can't do anything about their fate, so they might as well not worry about it. He isn't just encouraging them to keep a stiff upper lip or to look at the bright side of things. He is telling them that they have a very well-founded reason not to worry. The Father is diligently, actively looking out for their interests.

Peter knew that. The same apostle who slept in prison one tumultuous night quoted a well-known psalm in one of his letters several years later: "Cast all your anxiety on him because he cares for you."[2] He had heard Jesus command the disciples not to worry, he had been delivered out of several storms by Jesus' word, he had been miraculously rescued from prison twice, and he had seen God's sovereign hand guiding the church's affairs. But he had also suffered persecution and seen fellow believers die, so he wasn't naive about the costs of faith. Still, he trusted God. He knew from experience that in every situation, at every moment, in every way, God was taking care of his children because Jesus had said emphatically that he would.

Do you see the absurdity of our stress? We are very busy and anxious about the very things God has already said he's taking care of. We are relentless in our pursuit of what he has already promised to deliver. We micromanage the concerns we've allegedly asked him to handle. That's about as ludicrous as a confirmed lottery winner anxiously watching the news to see if his number will come up. God has already guaranteed what we need. What are we worried about?

I know where our minds frequently go from here. We know deep down inside that Jesus has promised that God will give us what we need, but we want so much more. We want to maintain a reasonably comfortable lifestyle, send our kids to the right schools, achieve great things for God and his glory, take a decent vacation, get a better job, and so on. We don't want the assurances that a bunch of subsistence farmers and craftsmen received a couple thousand years ago. That essentially amounts to a guarantee of enough goat's milk and figs to keep us alive, and that doesn't exactly soothe our worries. We want the twenty-first-century version of the Sermon on the Mount, and we just aren't sure Jesus' promises translate to a Western, economically advanced culture. We want him to tell us that God will take care of our needs on a scale relative to the rest of our society, not on a scale relative to first-century Galilee. For the most part, we aren't traumatized by the threat of not surviving; we're traumatized by the threat of losing the status quo we've worked hard to maintain.

Even so, Jesus says not to worry. Period. Why? Because we have a very good reason not to. This is still a well-founded promise regardless of the economic conditions in which it was first presented. I happen to think, both from biblical evidence and my own experience, that Jesus' words translate to our culture, too, even though we aren't hanging on the edge of hardship quite as much as first-century Jews were. God understands that we want to achieve, to send our kids to great schools, to be salt and light in the suburbs as well as the inner city, and to get a higher degree or a better job. Sure, he may shift us out of our status quo sometimes, and we have to fully expect that he might. But only for great purposes ordained by him. If you read Jesus' teaching carefully enough, the gist of it isn't, "Don't worry; God will keep you alive by a thread"; it's, "Don't worry, your Father loves to bless his children, and he has his eye on you." After all,

God lavishes the miracle of flight and extraordinary beauty on small wildlife and plants. Surely he lavishes generosity on his children, too.

When we really get this, we relinquish our fear, which frees us up to seek God above all else. We can be totally pre-occupied with the things of his Kingdom because "all these things"—the necessities of life—will be added to those who fully invest themselves in eternity. We have to understand that he is devoted to putting us in the right places at the right times and stocking us with all we need for all he has called us to do. We have to be able to rest in that fact. Any stress about whether or not Jesus will take care of us is a stark rebuttal to his words. Somehow we got comfortable with being living contradictions: Christians who "believe" in the words of Jesus but worry anyway. That makes no sense.

The Sermon on the Mount isn't the only time Jesus urged us to live an unburdened life. Just as well known is his plea to the tired and burned-out: "Come to me, all of you who are weary and carry heavy burdens, and I will give you rest."[3] Those words had less to do with the basic needs of life; they were directed more toward people stressed about having a right relationship with God. Religion can be a huge burden, placing demands on us that are clearly higher than our ability to accomplish. It puts ideals in front of us that we long to embrace but can never reach, at least not in our own effort. Striving to live a spiritually fruitful life in the strength of the flesh is a never-ending pursuit. Obedience, in its truest and fullest sense, eludes us. But even that, said Jesus, isn't a matter for anxiety—not for those who come to him. He is gentle and humble. He gives rest for our souls.

Most Christians love that verse, but it's yet another example of something we "believe" and still exhibit great stress over. We either strain to live a life of impact for God, or we assume that if he doesn't want us to worry about it, his calling must not be that extreme or compelling to begin with. Few of us get to a point of fully embracing both the radical nature of discipleship *and* the radical empowerment of the Spirit within us. But it's possible to be a Spirit-filled radical who isn't crushed under the weight of being a disciple and impacting the world for Christ. Those who come to Jesus in the way he calls can bear an enormous responsibility for changing the world and never be stressed about it.

> **Few of us get to a point of fully embracing both the radical nature of discipleship *and* the radical empowerment of the Spirit within us.**

Scripture includes plenty of references to this kind of life. "Give your burdens to the LORD, and he will take care of you," said a psalmist.[4] "Don't worry about anything," Paul exhorted.[5] "Let us strip off every weight that slows us down . . . and let us run with endurance the race God has set before us," the writer of the book of Hebrews urged.[6] "Those who trust in the LORD will find new strength. They will soar high on wings like eagles. They will run and not grow weary. They will walk and not faint," wrote a great prophet.[7] In fact, the sheer number of occurrences of "do not fear" and "do not worry" in the Bible is staggering. Clearly, there is some quality of life, some sense of freedom, some level of energy that people are meant to have. We were designed to soar.

Having Burdens without Bearing Them

This doesn't mean, of course, that the Christian life is like cruising down the highway on summer break with the wind in your hair. The feeling I described at the beginning of this chapter was based on my lack of obligations, not a supernatural energy to carry the ones I had. But I'm convinced that I can experience that same feeling of freedom in almost any situation now, at least to some degree. I believe we were meant to be unburdened.

Let me explain what I *don't* mean by that. Some people pursue the unburdened life by adopting a laid-back lifestyle and a "life's a beach" mentality. They refuse to get too attached to anyone or anything. They pursue pleasure and comfort with as little effort and concern as possible. They may work hard, but only so they can take time off and party harder. Responsibility is only a temporary necessity to put up with between the lighter moments of life. That is, in fact, one way to be unburdened, but it isn't a spiritual ideal.

Others pursue the unburdened life in a more spiritually sophisticated way. One of the major goals of Buddhism is detachment. Because human desires and passions are the source of pain and suffering, the way to "salvation" is to get rid of all desires and passions. The path to enlightenment is to escape from individuality—a complete denial of self, though not in the Christian sense—a process that takes multiple lifetimes to achieve. That, too, is one way to become unburdened. But that isn't what Jesus was talking about either.

There are a lot of counterfeit ways to live with less weight, but they aren't ultimately satisfying. The gospel doesn't lead to a "don't worry, be happy" lifestyle. It isn't simply about shedding all responsibilities and obligations in order to be unencumbered—though God often leads us to streamline our lives for more single-minded service. It doesn't make us apathetic or uncaring. The unburdened life is not a matter of "chilling out" or becoming "laid-back" in pursuit of the ideal personality. And it isn't about having all the conveniences and comforts we can afford in order to take it easy—or about saving up for them so we can retire in peace. It's about a godly way to live life with less effort and under less weight.

But is that even feasible—or, for that matter, biblical? After all, we're told to bear one another's burdens.[8] Paul was "burdened" for his churches.[9] Prophets like Ezekiel and Jeremiah were weighed down with extremely serious messages from God to his people, and they suffered greatly to carry those messages. Jeremiah, for example, had two options: to let the fire in his bones burn with the unspoken warnings of God, or to speak the warnings and bear the wrath of his kinsmen. Ezekiel saw traumatic visions, acted out extremely uncomfortable prophecies, and watched his wife die for the sake of God's message to his people. Were they missing out on the unburdened life they could have had?

Likewise, history is full of people who went to extraordinary lengths and endured extreme hardship to take the gospel to new places or to blaze new trails in the church's methods and ministries around the world. Many of them were ridiculed or even killed for confronting the world's sins or violating the religious traditions of the church. They suffered pain and rejection for the sake of God's Word. Were they missing out on a biblical ideal of living weightlessly?

Many Christians can testify to the pain of being "burdened" with prayers of intercession. They have withstood many sleepless nights and forgone numerous meals in order to do business in unseen realms for the sake of

> There's a difference between the kind of burden God places on a person's shoulders to carry in his strength and the burden that overwhelms and crushes a person's spirit, miring him or her in futility.

the lost and the God who loves them. Are they just naive and spiritually immature enough to have missed a vital biblical truth of being unburdened?

No, of course not. Persecution and toil are not light matters in the Kingdom of God. But nearly every one of those people affirms that there's a difference between the kind of burden God places on a person's shoulders to carry in his strength and the kind of burden that overwhelms and crushes a person's spirit, miring him or her in futility. Some burdens are oppressive, and some are supernaturally carried.

That's why it's possible for someone like Isaiah to preach a hard message to a stubborn nation, encounter oppressive resistance to it, and still talk about soaring with wings like an eagle's. That's why David could suffer the consequences of his own sin, endure the deepest pains of family dysfunction, fight for his life in numerous battles against a multitude of enemies, and still praise God for renewing his youth, setting him on high places, and fulfilling his heart's desires. And that's why Paul could write about all his shipwrecks and beatings and opponents and still break out in gratitude for the inexpressible joy of serving God and identifying with Jesus. These people were able to carry extraordinary weight because they had learned the principle of resting in a supernatural source, often by sheer necessity. They had borne burdens, but not without help. The unburdened life isn't so much about avoiding burdens as it is about carrying them with the strength of Another. The former leads to a life of purposelessness; the latter builds an eternal Kingdom. The first approach is a choice to be weak; the other is a choice to be supernaturally empowered. This isn't a matter simply of living with abandonment, but of living with abandonment *to God.*

Transcending a Storm

Jesus made the disciples get in a boat and go to the other side of the lake.[10] He compelled them, forced them, ordered them, apparently against their will. Why didn't they want to go? We don't know. Maybe they knew the conditions were unstable. Perhaps they were perfectly willing to get into the boat but wanted him to come with them rather than head off to the hills to pray. Or maybe they were just tired after a long season of ministry and would have preferred to rest where they were. Regardless of the reason, Jesus made them go.

They probably weren't thrilled with his seeming lack of foresight when a storm came up. Such storms weren't unusual; the Sea of Galilee was known for its sudden squalls. And while this storm may not have been as bad as others the disciples had to endure, it still required quite a bit of effort to keep control of the boat. The wind was strong, the waves were heavy, and it was late at night. They had just absorbed the news of John the Baptist's death and dealt with thousands of people hungry for miracles and food. Now, likely exhausted, they were getting tossed around by merciless waves.

To make matters worse, they were accosted by a phantom, a specter hovering on the water at three in the morning. Fishermen have their tales—legends of spooky encounters from the unknown deeps—but these men weren't counting on being part of any such story. Nevertheless, the spirit neared. They literally screamed in terror.

Jesus spoke immediately to relieve their fears. He announced his presence, assured them that he was no ghost, and told them not to be afraid. Unconvinced, Peter asked for confirmation. "If it's really you, tell me to come to you, walking on the water." It was a bizarre request. Perhaps he thought he had nothing to lose; if it was really Jesus, the feat would prove it, and if this was a ghost, he might as well drown. Regardless, he had the nerve to ask, and Jesus honored his nerve with an answer. "Yes, come."

It had to feel good at first. This mortal man of real flesh and blood and at least average weight was walking on a substance much less dense than he was. He had floated on water before with the help of a boat, but he had never transcended it. To him, as to nearly every Jew, deep water represented chaos and danger. It was to be feared by most and at least respected by those who had to earn their living on it. Unlike Phoenicians and other seafaring people of the ancient Near East, Jews considered the seas to be a dark mystery far from the Spirit of God.[11] Now the Son of God was walking on one, and so was a common fisherman. This was not only a miracle; it was a paradigm shift of epic proportions.

Sadly, the exhilaration was brief. Peter took his eyes off Jesus and stared instead at the chaos around him: strong wind and huge waves. In a dramatic picture featured prominently in the preaching of nearly every pulpit speaker since, Peter lost his focus. The results were immediate. While empowered by his gaze at the Savior, Peter defied physics. When fed instead by the threats around him, Peter plummeted. One mental posture set him on top of his circumstances; the other forced him to submit to them. Both before and after Peter's descent, the circumstances were the same—nothing about the wind and waves changed. Jesus didn't calm the storm so Peter could tread on water; the feat would have been impossible in any weather conditions other than a deep freeze. No, the situation was the same throughout the entire story. The sea was tumultuous. The only things that changed were Peter's focus, his level of fear, and his ability to overcome his environment.

That's an accurate portrait of the contrast between the unburdened life and its discouraging alternative. The difference between them has nothing to do with getting our issues to go away. We aren't going to be able to have a carefree existence by getting rid of our cares. That isn't an option. The wind and the waves are inevitable. Our only choice is whether to sink under our circumstances or rise above them. And according to biblical truth and the promises of God, rising above them is a very real possibility. Walking on water in the midst of a storm is a genuine alternative.

I've often wondered why God doesn't just give us the carefree life we dream of. Why doesn't he take away the issues and problems that plague us when we come to him in faith? Why do we still have to go through the same difficulties as before? As I was preparing to write this section, the father of a friend's friend died without ever having received Christ, even though he had been the subject of many prayers over many years. Isn't that a heavy burden worth grieving over? Another friend has a terminally ill mother who has needed extensive long-term care by family members who are pretty well exhausted by now. Is that not a cause for stress? Several of my colleagues were laid off recently because gifts to nonprofit ministries like ours drop dramatically during an economic crisis. These kinds of things are the backdrop behind Jesus' promises and, if we're honest, the source of most of our doubts when we hear a seemingly blithe command like, "Do not worry about your life." Don't worry? Are you kidding, Lord? You never promise to take such excruciating pain away from us, and yet you tell us not to worry?

It seems unrealistic, doesn't it? And it would be—if God didn't step in with supernatural strength to be able to handle such circumstances. But I think that's one of the main reasons he doesn't just remove all adversity from us when we come to him in faith and ask for help. He leaves us in the midst of our adversity for a reason, not so we can be overcome by it, but so we can overcome it in him. There's a strange and remarkable interplay between our needs and God's supply in which he gets glorified by stepping into our circumstances and carrying our burdens for us. He doesn't take the burdens away, but he lightens them by his strength. He becomes the bearer as we present them to him. And in the process, he gets to show who he is.

Think about that. God was able to show himself as Israel's Deliverer only because he allowed his people to be slaves in Egypt in the first place. He showed himself as their Provider only because he led them into a wilderness that had no water or food to sustain them. He showed himself as Healer only when they were allowed to experience disease and as their Warrior only when they had an enemy. The overwhelming circumstances in the history of his chosen people became the platform for his revelation. We would not know who he is today if somebody, somewhere, sometime had not had a deep need that he stepped in and met.

This is an ongoing dynamic. God's character wasn't on display just for one season or among one group of people. He still reveals himself in our lives and in the lives of people around us, primarily through our needs and his ability to meet them. We may know him theoretically as Israel's Deliverer, Provider, Healer, and Warrior, but we know him personally only if he performs those roles in our lives when we need him to. And that's why he doesn't remove the wind and waves from our lives. We can sink and suffer among them, or we can find his strength and walk on them. But that carefree life we long for—that feeling I had on that drive home from college—can't be attained by perpetually calm waters. Not now, not in this world. The only way to live the unburdened life is by having difficulties and learning how to rely on God to deal with them.

> We may know God theoretically as Israel's Deliverer, Provider, Healer, and Warrior, but we know him personally by these names only if he performs those roles in our lives.

That's why this kind of life seems so elusive. If you're like me, you keep looking for that season of calm waters, that ideal situation when no sticky relationships are clamoring for attention, no needs are pressing down on you, no deadlines are urgently screaming at you, no bills are mocking your inability to pay them, no health problems are nagging at you, and your workload is uncharacteristically sane. That season may come for brief moments and in varying degrees, but it will never be a way of life in this age. What *can* be a way of life is the ability to nearly effortlessly carry burdens that would be crushing to most people. How? By faith. By a refusal to worry and a commitment to prayer. By allowing the Spirit of God to live within you and not only give you strength but *be* your strength.

That's the goal. The rest of this book will focus on the means to the end. We'll examine the source of our burdens: why we have them, where they come from, and how deeply they've grown roots in our lives. We'll look at the many ways—some of them surprising—that we carry unnecessary weight, as well as what it really means to shift the responsibility of our baggage off our own shoulders and onto shoulders much greater and more capable than ours. We'll explore why it's so difficult to let go of the things we cling to, even the things we desperately want to get rid of. And we'll find out what freedom really means and how we can maintain it.

The unburdened life is a calling to carry exactly what God places on our shoulders—nothing more, nothing less, nothing else—in the strength that he gives us. It can look to others like a hard path to climb, but it can feel as effortless as a sailboat being blown by the wind. We can't do that unless we make some key decisions and shift the way we think. But it can be done. According to Jesus and the experience of many who know him, it's possible. In fact, it's necessary. It's the way we're designed to live.

CHAPTER 2

ROOTS

FOR AS LONG as he could remember, Glenn wanted to be a doctor. In his family, that's how little boys grew up to be heroes. It was the ultimate means of earning honor and respect. Since Glenn was thirsty for honor and respect, that's exactly what he set his mind to do. And he didn't just want to be an ordinary doctor, although his parents would have been amply pleased with that. He wanted to be a highly specialized surgeon. The best in his field. The expert to whom lesser experts looked for advice and inspiration. He would make his parents, his siblings, his grandparents—and especially himself—very, very proud.

Glenn knew that in order to achieve his goals, he would

have to study extremely hard. He relentlessly pursued the kind of grades that would get him to one of the finest universities in the country. Once there, he zealously and single-mindedly earned the kind of grades that would get him into the finest medical school for his specialty. The only distraction he allowed himself was dating the girlfriend who would eventually become his wife. That's because marriage and family were also an integral part of the picture that would make his parents, siblings, grandparents, and himself proud. But aside from the necessary search for a mate, he focused entirely on his future career.

Toward the end of college, Glenn found the pace of his life and the intensity of his focus exhausting. He couldn't give up his dream, though, because his dream had become his identity. But he wasn't sure he could achieve it without wearing himself out. So he occasionally popped some stimulants while preparing for big exams. "Occasionally" soon turned into "regularly," which soon turned into "habitually" and "almost obsessively." And it worked—after graduating with high honors, he was accepted into a top med school, where he continued his relentless pace with his "extra help" for the next several years. In fact, he continued relying on it throughout residency and then into his practice. He was excellent at what he did—and thoroughly stressed out about it.

Glenn had achieved his dream—sort of—at least in the sense of establishing the identity he wanted and making everyone proud. But his lifestyle prevented him from being the kind of husband and father he wanted to be; there were simply too many pieces of this dream to try to fit together. His marriage was superficial, his enormous debts from medical school demanded greater devotion to work, his kids barely knew him, and his addictions grew stronger and more diverse. On the outside, he had become what he wanted to be. On the inside, he was overwhelmed by his own responsibilities, his drive to carry them out exceedingly well, and his deep-down awareness that he was failing in the things that really mattered in life. It was a no-win situation.

Glenn eventually found himself sitting in a substance-abuse treatment center with his sterling reputation in tatters, divorce papers awaiting his signature, and his extended family in shock over how someone so gifted and blessed could have so carelessly thrown it all away. From all outward appearances, he had simply risen to the top and then let his pride get the best of him. Few knew that he was just a little boy who had tried to earn the admiration of everyone around him and ultimately failed.

> **We jump from one activity, endeavor, or relationship to another trying to scratch itches that we can't even identify.**

Sadly, that isn't an unusual story. Most of us are driven to seek our own fulfillment, often to cover up or compensate for the wounds of childhood. We may not be quite so driven in our quests or crash quite so dramatically as Glenn did, but we're all seeking something. We find ourselves filled with an insatiable desire to be loved, to achieve, to find peace, and to have our desires met. So we jump from one activity, endeavor, or relationship to another trying to scratch itches that we can't even identify. The outward manifestations of our aspirations include

- materialism, which can be an unhealthy pursuit of comfort or a sign of constant dissatisfaction with life;
- workaholism, which can come from an excessive need to achieve or from a desire to avoid other issues;
- meaningless or superficial relationships, which can come from a fear of attachment or commitment or from a need to constantly be affirmed by someone new;
- codependent relationships, which can come from a fear of being lonely or suffering rejection;
- addictions to food, drugs, or sex, which can serve as an anesthesia for pain, a substitute for love and acceptance, an excuse for failure, or an escape from difficult issues.

This is a very general, brief, and incomplete list of the many possible ways to cover our wounds and strive for fulfillment, but can you see some common results? They all do nothing to relieve us of our burdens. In fact, without exception, they complicate our lives and actually add more burdens to them. They cause us to get caught up in an exhausting rat race, place extraordinary demands on our time and energy, create more problems to solve (or to feel guilty about ignoring), drain us of money, destroy our physical and emotional health, and enslave us to hard-to-break, self-damaging habits that can have long-term repercussions. Our desperate search for fulfillment drives us in exactly the opposite direction of where we want to go. The result is a heavy, burdensome existence.

Where It Began

Our cravings for approval, status, love, and peace weren't part of our original design. The need for those things was, but we had them all in Eden. In innocence, our first parents had no hunger to earn the approval of their Creator or each other; approval was already implied. It would not have occurred to them to seek a higher status or to search for a greater love than they already knew. There were no conflicts to overcome or wounds to compensate for. They had all they needed. Stress didn't even enter the picture.

Something drastic happened at the Fall. We lost our identity, our security, and our position. God was still watching over us, but our relationship with him was fractured. We were under his care, but not within the safety of the Garden. We lost sight of who we are and focused on new concerns like survival. Our personalities had to adapt to a strange new sense of shame. Our instincts began to function from the basis of fear. We entered a competitive, high-stakes, every-man-for-himself environment. Instead of just being, we began wandering. Instead of exercising dominion over the earth, we began scraping to get by. Instead of living in victory, we got a taste of futility. We became alienated and insecure. And in order to compensate for our alienation and insecurity, we became emotionally needy and self-seeking.

Jesus came to save us from all of that, but it's hard to leave a life of anxieties and insecurities behind us. The only way we can is to fully embrace the redemption he offers, and that often takes time. Even after we accept him as our Savior, those wounds and fears that motivate us linger. As a result, instead of receiving the extravagant love and acceptance of God, we desperately seek affirmation through the approval that comes with status and accomplishments; we try to establish our security through savings and other protective measures; and we try to find love through dependent, unhealthy relationships. We want the world and the people around us to fill up all those things that are lacking deep in our souls.

Do you see the problem? This desperate search for fulfillment is a burden in itself, but it also fills our lives with numerous other burdens that we try to balance and maintain as though our lives depended on it. We stress about our finances and our relationships and the direction of our lives and even our survival because deep down inside, we desperately need all these things to be somebody. They shape our identities in unnatural ways. We have nagging fears that if we lose the props we've come to depend on, we will lose the core of ourselves, the essence of who we are. The result is a lot of worry and stress.

This desperate search multiplies when we are really close to the people we love. We find, for example, that we not only feel the pressure of fulfilling our own lives, but also those of our spouses and children. If others in our lives are hurting or empty, we feel the pain of their wounds as much as if those wounds were our own. Their craving for fulfillment gets wrapped up in ours. The result is even greater degrees of anxiety.

Don't get me wrong. It's healthy to want strong relationships and success. The problem is in how we define those things and the degree to which our fears and loneliness seize upon them as though they were life to us. A desire for well-being is good; an obsession about well-being that keeps us awake at night is not. In the redemption Jesus has given us, our desires have been met. Our needs will be taken care of. There is therefore no reason for our obsessions to weigh us down.

God's original design for us was simplicity. He gave us the work of tending Eden

> A desire for well-being is good; an obsession about well-being that keeps us awake at night is not.

and subduing the earth, so he didn't create us for laziness and comfort. In fact, at moderate levels and for certain purposes, stress is a valuable aspect of our design. But God did seem to place only reasonable expectations and obligations on us. We were given manageable responsibilities and offered an uncomplicated relationship with him and others. We don't know exactly how these relationships and responsibilities would have developed if Eden had remained Eden, but we can see how they were distorted and complicated by the Fall. Sin, futility, and death play huge parts in our lives today. We go through life with stresses we were never meant to have. Many of those stresses come from a misperception of God and our role in this world.

Myth of the Hard Master

Toward the end of his ministry, Jesus told his followers a parable about his return. It would be like a man who went on a journey, leaving his possessions with his servants to handle as they saw fit. He gave five talents to one servant, two talents to another, and one talent to a third. The first two invested the money and saw it double over time. The third allowed his fear to take control and buried his money in order to preserve it.[1]

Why did the third servant behave differently than the other two? Perhaps because he saw the master as "a hard man," he couldn't bring himself to trust in the master's mercy in the unfortunate event of possible failure. As a result, he felt a lot of pressure to hang on to what he had been given. But this attitude earned no respect from Jesus. The first two servants, who were willing to risk everything—the entire sum they had been given—were called "good and faithful" and entered into the joy of the master. The third was thrown into the darkness where there's weeping and gnashing of teeth. Whether this refers to ultimate judgment or the painful regret of missed opportunities, the picture is sobering. Those who seemed inspired by the trust they were given were rewarded. The one who was paralyzed by the responsibility was rejected. And each one's perception of the master determined the difference.

Though this passage is often used to make a point about tithing, it's so much broader than that. For one thing, the servants invested *all* their money, not a tenth of it, so this parable clearly applies to more of life than just our Sunday offerings. It relates to everything God gives us and how we leverage it for his purposes. We can trust God to give us the resources he wants us to have, and we can invest those resources enthusiastically in his Kingdom without fear of loss or rebuke. In faith, we can lay ourselves completely on the line without fear of missing his best for our lives.

This parable has profound significance for our relationship with God. The reason we strive so hard to fill all our own needs is because we aren't sure he's going to do that for us. We don't know that we will get what we need from him. We try to soothe our wounds with possessions and status and food and pleasure and relationships because we haven't let our wounds be healed by him. The fundamental question behind that problem is this: Is God a hard master? In other words, can we really trust him?

The answer to that second question, of course, is yes. The servants who pleased the master most in the parable were the ones who seemed to have the least amount of stress and the greatest amount of confidence that their master was good. The one who hoarded—an appropriate metaphor for how we hang on to our burdens—assumed he had to. His master was "hard," after all, so who knew whether he would ever get another coin? Because he wasn't sure how generous his boss was, the servant tried to hold on to what he had. And that, said Jesus, leads to weeping and gnashing of teeth. This idea of the "hard master" can permeate our lives, and the more it affects us, the more burdened we feel. If we were completely confident in God's love, we wouldn't worry about the approval of others—and we certainly wouldn't try to earn brownie points in his eyes or worry about losing them whenever we stumble. If we were completely confident in his provision, we wouldn't constantly hedge against disaster. If we were completely confident in his wisdom, we wouldn't lie awake at night wondering "what if" about every possible contingency to every possible event in our lives. And if we were completely confident that he has good plans for us and wants us to be thoroughly fulfilled in him, we would drop our desperate designs for our own fulfillment. That search is exhausting—and, according to Scripture, completely unnecessary for those who trust in God.

I don't mean to give the impression that our sense of being burdened is always a product of a distorted, dysfunctional past. There are legitimate responsibilities that weigh us down, especially if we have a high degree of responsibility at work or in our family structure. Every good boss genuinely cares for the welfare of his or her employees. Every parent is burdened for his or her children at least to some degree out of love, not necessarily out of past wounds.[2] These relationships can create a certain amount of stress. And, it should be noted, stress isn't always bad. It usually isn't comfortable, but we were designed to feel it and be motivated by it in certain situations and in measured degrees. At the right times in the right ways, it can be very useful.

Even so, the high degree of stress we have from our responsibilities is unnecessary when we truly rely on the goodness of God to sovereignly guide us. Are we worried that he will take care of us but not help us handle our obligations? That he will give us what we need but not enough to give other people what they need? That he will watch over us but give us no wisdom or guidance for people under our charge? That makes no sense. We have to be aware that he is not only taking care of us but also the people we love or feel responsible for. He is not a hard master in their lives either. He will use us to care for them, but he will not let them go if we fail. There's freedom and rest in knowing that.

Anti-Worship on a Sleepless Night

Every time I see Jesus' assurances in the Sermon on the Mount that we don't need to worry, certain doubts go through my mind—those "yes, buts" that we tend to ask when we accept a basic statement but can think of a lot of variables it doesn't cover. I've become convinced that behind every "yes, but . . ." that I can think of is this idea of God being a hard master.

- "Sure, he promises to meet all my needs, but how does he define 'needs'?"
- "Sure, he promises to forgive all my sin, but what if he disciplines me harshly for it tomorrow by depriving me of something I want?"
- "Sure, he says he loves me, but he loves everyone . . . and a lot of people loved by him go through some really hard things."

You see what I mean? There's a "hard master" behind every one of those statements. I woke up in the middle of the night recently and lay awake for three hours. I wasn't planning to worry, I was planning to go back to sleep right away. It didn't happen. My mind started wandering, and wander turned to worry rather easily. It was about a legitimate concern of substantial importance—it always is. But lying awake was not a very effective way to deal with it.

We have all done that—most of us, anyway. The capacity for the human mind to consider possible threats to our well-being is enormous. We don't seem to consider that most of the threats we worry about never occur. We want to be prepared for the ones that do. Not that there's anything we can do about them, usually. We just don't want to be surprised.

Meanwhile, while we're trying to prepare ourselves mentally for everything that could possibly go wrong, we often live under a low level of stress and anxiety that wreaks havoc on our physical and emotional well-being. It's a true cultural phenomenon—people are stressed out. Insurance companies and doctors of many specialties verify it. We carry an awful load of burdens just by thinking about them.

People of Western cultures consume mood-altering pills at an amazing rate. And while there is certainly an appropriate chemical approach to problems of depression and anxiety, the problems seem to be magnified by two seemingly unstoppable trends: a world of increasing danger and a society with a decreasing ability to cope. While we can't do much on an individual level about the first trend, the second is entirely up to us. We have to figure out how to cope—how to avoid lying awake in the middle of the night wondering what might go wrong.

Already vulnerable in our stress and anxiety, we might be even more alarmed to find out that worry is sin. Does that seem harsh? Perhaps, but Jesus doesn't mince words. Including the repeated phrase "do not worry" in the Sermon on the Mount, he clearly says not to worry at least eight times.[3] And as I've mentioned, "Do not be afraid"—or some variation of it—is the most frequent command in the entire Bible.

Clearly, worry and anxiety are violations of God's command. But acknowledging this hardly seems a relaxing remedy. In fact, on top of our anxieties about life, knowing the sinfulness of our worries can cause us to worry even more. That's not God's intention, of course, because he isn't a hard master. This is a command that is meant to relax those who have cast their lot with him. It is to relieve us from the responsibility of figuring out the future and planning for every contingency. It is meant to remind us that God is sovereign, he is good, and his watchful eye is on those who trust him.

Why is worry sinful? Look at it this way. What would it say about me as a father if my ten-year-old constantly wondered where his next meal was coming from? Or if he lived in fear for his safety? Barring some unusual psychological disorder, his anxiety would probably indicate that he didn't put much stock in his father's character. Perhaps some fathers deserve that mistrust. God doesn't. His character is impeccable. But we worry anyway. What does that say about him? Or, more to the point, what does that say of what we think about him? It says we think he's a hard master.

That tells me we mentally assent to the truths of the gospel and God's promises of fatherhood, but we don't really believe them. In a sense, it's an emotional slander of his reputation—a defamation of his character. It's certainly not worship, which affirms God's goodness and power and wisdom. Worry doesn't reflect who God actually is; it's anti-worship, a form of lying about him.

> **Worry doesn't reflect who God actually is; it's anti-worship, a form of lying about him.**

Worry is also an affront to biblical revelation. Think about it. When we worry, we are saying, in effect, "God says his faithfulness is great, but I'm not so sure. He says he is a very present help in trouble, but that may not be entirely reliable. He says he covers our sins and has mercy on us, but maybe he's holding my mess over my head this time." Our anxiety is a contradiction of biblical truths. But the truth of the Bible is unassailable. It is our anxiety, not the Word, that is built on faulty premises. Though our worry is entirely unreliable, we often trust it more. We act as if God's mercy depends on whether we deserve it or not. We place fickle gut feelings over the immutable Word of God. That's no way to live.

We do that for a number of reasons, most of them involving that desperate search for fulfillment that we took upon ourselves after Eden. In addition, somewhere in the back of our minds, we know that God has let some really faithful people go through some really difficult times. He's quite honest about that. It's right there in our Bibles, and we've seen it in our own experiences. Our worries are really indications that we're afraid he'll do the same with us. Never mind that it might be for our greater glory in the grand eternal scheme of things. Never mind that it might be momentary pain for others' eternal benefit. Never mind that he promises to be right there with us every step of the way and to give us more than enough grace for the situation. Our instinct is to shy away from difficulty. If being in the center of God's will sometimes means pain for us, our spirits may be willing, but the flesh is weak. And the flesh is where all the worry is. We shrink back from the God of all comfort, hoping never to be in a position of needing it.

Intellectually, it helps me to know that worry is sin. I can deny anxiety and refuse to feel guilty about my lack of concern. If Jesus tells me not to worry about the future, I can live in the present without fear of being irresponsible. If someone tells me I'm not preoccupied enough with a situation, I can say, "Sorry, I'm just trying to be obedient." I must plan, of course, but I mustn't worry. I'm commanded not to do something I hate doing anyway. That's a relief.

But the emotional side is harder. Real discipleship can be like a roller coaster. We want the excitement of following Jesus and being part of God's plan. And we know it will turn out all right. But we panic on the twists and plunges anyway. The unexpected bends alarm us. Unlike the roller coaster, however, panic in discipleship is not part of the fun—it's a statement against the operator's faithfulness. We have to constantly remind ourselves that everyone who believes in him gets to the end of the ride just fine. He makes sure of it.

And that's our solution. That's how we can emotionally get past the worry—we worship. It's simple, but effective. We'll dig much deeper into that later, but it helps to remind ourselves of the faithfulness of the operator. We praise him for his presence, his promises, and his peace. We spend more time dwelling on how big God is than on how big our problems are. As we do, he becomes our stress-free preoccupation. He is not a hard master. He is a mighty, merciful Savior with an awesome track record.

Sometimes it's an act of worship just to go back to sleep.

That's what I'm going to think about the next time I find

myself lying awake at night—our mighty, merciful Savior. Sometimes it's an act of worship just to go back to sleep.

Shalom

Hebrew has a word for what we lost in Eden: *shalom*. It's the word we normally translate as "peace," but it means much more than that. It doesn't refer simply to a lack of conflict, the way we talk about peace today as an end to war or controversy. It's the fullness of God's Kingdom—the abundance, health, wholeness, completeness, safety, and prosperity in all of life that comes from being with God.

This is what we long for. This is what all the wheels spinning around in our minds are trying to figure out how to get. We want the fullness and the abundance of the Kingdom. When Paul wrote of all creation groaning for its redemption,[4] this is what we're groaning for. We know deep down that something is tragically wrong, and the desperate search that unwittingly piles burdens onto our shoulders is an attempt to fix it. We want that "all is well" satisfaction with life, that place of blessing that makes us feel free and content. That longing is a distant echo from the Garden. The burdens we impose on ourselves are futile attempts to get the echo to stop making such unsettling noise.

When the Bible speaks of Jesus as our peace,[5] the means to peace,[6] or the Prince of Peace,[7] it's telling us that he is our Shalom. The Redeemer does his work on that deep-seated place where the wounds and the emptiness are. He doesn't just reconcile us to God in the sense that our sins are now overlooked; he does a profound healing in the depths where we long for Eden. The source of our worry and stress has become the object of his rescue plan. He has come to settle whatever unsettles us.

We need to know that. I don't think we can completely understand it or even observe the process of how he fills our empty places, but we need to know that this is his agenda. This is his heart. He has a solution for all the obscure, festering sources of those cravings that cause us to add so much weight to our lives. He has a plan for the source of all those things that keep us up at night. All of those reasons we develop our agendas and try to work out our own lives are made impotent by something he does deep within us.

I'm not sure exactly what's involved in that, but I know it includes a few vital facts:

- *He assures us we are totally accepted in him.* Our need to fill our lives with fake loves or obsessive loves is undone.
- *He assures us he is zealous about his care for us.* Our tendency to worry about our futures and arrange our own security is unnecessary.
- *He assures us that we will ultimately be fulfilled.* Our desire to satisfy all our cravings however we see fit is misguided.
- *He assures us that he is totally trustworthy and dependable in all that he says and does.* Our musings

about whether his promises are guarded by legal
loopholes or fine-print disclaimers are unfounded.

The reason we can feel unburdened is that Jesus is making
the weightiness of life unnecessary. He isn't suddenly declaring important things unimportant or denying the serious-
ness of real issues, but he
is unplugging our sense of
responsibility for soothing
our own wounds, building
our own kingdoms, earning
our own loves, and establish-
ing our own identities. He comes to save us, not to assist
us. He doesn't deny that we have heavy issues to deal with.
He simply offers to take all of our weighty matters onto his
own shoulders and let us rest in him. Our search for fulfillment is no longer on our to-do list. It's on his. We can shift
from depending on our own resources and schedules and
agendas to depending on his plans for us. And that's how we
can be unburdened. In his mercy, he promises to give us his
shalom.

Our search for fulfillment is no longer on our to-do list. It's on his.

The Rest of Mercy

We talk about God's mercy a lot, but we rarely actually
embrace it. Yet only when we do can we find true rest. The
way to an unburdened life begins deep inside a heart that
can look back to the Garden of Eden in Genesis, look ahead

to the City of God in Revelation, and focus in the here and now on how the Cross brings the God of the Garden and the City into our present circumstances. That deep place is where burdens begin to either grow lighter or leave us altogether.

Our sense of heaviness or lightness begins in the depths of our souls. When God's Spirit does not fill the emptiness there, we try to fill it with other things. That results in a lot of works, performance, self-effort, exalted agendas, and very busy schedules. But when his Spirit does fill the emptiness there, he works outward to accomplish through us the things he wants to accomplish. It's his strength, not ours, that does his will.

That means that if you feel inspired to build stronger relationships, accomplish great things, dream big dreams, and guard the security of your family, that's probably God working within you. But if you feel pressured to do these things as though your life depended on it, it probably isn't. God often gives us a holy discontentment to drive us forward and keep us seeking his will for our lives, but the source is his Spirit, not our wounds or our emptiness. The kind of discontentment that simply causes us to be restless, lose sleep, and desperately find ways to meet all our deepest needs is an unholy discontentment that comes from not understanding or believing what God has promised and secured for us. Until we can learn to tell the difference, we can't live an unburdened life.

Do you understand the implications of that? Think about it:

- That voice telling you that you absolutely have to maintain a certain amount in your savings and retirement accounts in order to be cared for in your old age is not God's voice. God can take care of you any way he chooses any time he chooses without any regard to conventional expectations and means. He is not governed by probabilities and patterns in your life or in the financial currents of the day. He can (and often does) work outside of them. He may lead you to save wisely, but he won't keep you up at night worrying about the market or a job loss.
- That voice telling you that you have to look and act a certain way and maintain a certain image in order to find the spouse of your dreams or have the right friends is not God's voice. God can bring the right people into your life at the right time however he wants to.
- That voice telling you that "if you don't have your health, you don't have anything," is not God's voice. Your outer body will eventually waste away.[8] Your inner spirit will forever grow stronger. God is deeply concerned for your body, and he does promise to heal us, but he is infinitely more invested in your heart. That's where his Spirit thrives and does amazing things in your life.
- That voice telling you that you missed your opportunities to live the life God wanted to give you and that he'll never use you the way he could have is not God's voice. Regrets are a heavy burden to bear,

and they don't take into account the redemption Jesus gives us. God can and does work all things together for the good of those who love him.[9]

- That voice that tells you that you're unlovable or unattractive or unworthy is not God's voice. There is nothing you can do to make yourself more accepted or loved by him—or less so. If you have come to him in faith, it's because he has chosen you. Why? Because he wanted to. Because he saw the good way your story ends and is committed to it.

- The voice that tells you that you might go through a difficult time . . . well, that one might actually be his. But the voice that tells you that difficult time will end in disaster or despair—or that says the difficulty might not be worth the trouble—is not God's voice. The hardships of his people never outweigh the blessings they'll receive for going through them. Never.

> **The hardships of God's people never outweigh the blessings they'll receive for going through them.**

This list could go on and on, you know. There are thousands of lying voices that weigh us down with pressures and concerns, but none of them fit God's purpose for our lives. Our desperate search for fulfillment is in the process of being satisfied, and the happy result is guaranteed. We are absolutely assured that our deepest longings in the core of our souls have been, are being, and will forever be met by Jesus. We may not feel it now or understand how that will work out, but it's true. There is nothing else to strive for, no desperate search to persist in, no greater love to secure, no higher status to attain. Everything we seek in his Kingdom can be pursued from a place of trust and rest.

A Lighter Life

The story of Glenn at the beginning of this chapter is a sobering illustration of how the desperate search for fulfillment can crush us. The following story, which a friend of mine included in his book, is a much lighter-hearted look at the same dynamic. Though no one seems to know the author or origin of this tale—my friend received it in an e-mail— it does a great job of showing how misguided some of our burdens can be.

An American businessman struck up a conversation with a fisherman in a small coastal Mexican village. Noticing his fairly small catch, the American asked why he didn't stay out longer and try for a bigger haul. The Mexican said he had enough to support his family's immediate needs.

"What do you do with the rest of your time?" the American asked.

"I sleep late; fish a little; play with my children; take a siesta with my wife, Maria; and stroll into the village each evening, where I sip wine and play guitar with my amigos. I have a full and busy life, señor."

"I am a Harvard MBA and could help you," said the scoffing American, who proceeded to advise him to buy a bigger boat and eventually a whole fleet, followed by a cannery, and then have enough money to move to a big city to run his expanding business empire.

"What then, señor?"

The American told him he'd be a millionaire.

"Then what, señor?"

"Then you would retire and move to a small coastal fishing village where you would sleep late, fish a little, play with your kids, take a siesta with your wife, and stroll to the village in the evenings, where you could sip wine and play your guitar with your amigos."[10]

Someone on a desperate search to soothe the wounds from Eden by making a name for himself or herself couldn't play the role of the fisherman in that story. But that fisherman isn't a bad example of what Jesus meant when he said not to worry. That doesn't mean God won't send some people into the corporate world to manage huge accounts and lots of personnel. He most certainly will. He will also send his people into impossible situations and nation-changing ministries. But when he does, it won't be with an unreasonable pressure to perform and produce out of their own natural resources and strength. His favor always follows his assignments. And his burdens are always light.

CHAPTER 3

LOADS

THERE ARE FEW perfect metaphors for life, but commuting on an urban interstate may be one of them. Masses of cars weave in and out of lanes, but they are usually moving in generally the same direction, and everyone seems to be headed somewhere. Some people want to get to their destinations in a hurry, and others seem just to enjoy the ride. Most know exactly where they want to go, but others don't seem to have a clue. Occasionally you'll see a driver who appears to be enjoying the adventure, but the vast majority are simply going through the motions and seem resigned to their daily routes.

On the highway, you'll see a few legalists who insist on

doing everything *exactly* by the rules, even when abiding by the letter of the law is more hazardous than following the spirit of it. But more people ignore the rules altogether— or at least the rules most convenient to ignore at any given moment. And some people are downright hypocritical, expecting everyone else to obey the law but honking at any hint of a suggestion that they should do the same.

As in life, some drivers are highly skilled and others aren't. Some use their gifts wisely; others, recklessly. Some are pushy tailgaters or rude line breakers; others are nice enough to let you in front of them. Some drivers give you a friendly wave, but most just mind their own business. Some people travel in groups; others, alone. You see a lot of pride and competition on the highway, as some people speed up just so you can't pass them. You see a lot of unfairness there, but law enforcers come along occasionally to make sure everything goes generally according to plan. Even so, sometimes tragedy occurs and halts someone prematurely at the side of the road.

You'll see rich vehicles and poor vehicles, healthy ones and sick ones, those that are well dressed and others that are a little disheveled, and even some that are seriously down-and-out. There's a diversity of shapes, sizes, and colors, and almost always an oddball or two to make things really interesting. The roads are sometimes smooth and sometimes rough, and occasionally you have to make an unexpected detour. Some days go pretty smoothly, and others seem bumper to bumper from beginning to end. But you can always find a commentator on the airwaves telling you how it's all going.

I've found that the morning commute, like life, can be pretty stressful. But I've also found that a lot of the stress comes from my own attitude toward other drivers. I get really offended, for example, at the pushy people who want to cut in front of me without signaling or gesturing (nicely) or warning me at all. My hostility toward them, which usually turns into disgust for the rudeness of the entire human race, can set me on edge before I ever get to work—even though their actions have set me back only by approximately two seconds. For some reason, I seem to think that a few seconds here and there make an enormous difference in how much I'm going to accomplish on any given day. Perhaps that's why I keep inching closer toward the bumper in front of me—a behavior that has been scientifically proven both to increase stress dramatically and to save absolutely no time whatsoever. I have perspectives and habits that add burdens without accomplishing anything good.

I like using the highways as a parable for life because nearly every human emotion can emerge when we're behind the wheel. We can relax and enjoy the breeze, get frustrated and curse at our problems, celebrate the sights we see and the passengers we're with, look at others with either compassion or anger, lament the minor tragedies of flat tires and the major tragedies of serious accidents, and so on. This metaphor has a way of putting my own issues into perspective. I've found that attitudes I stuff down in normal life come out much more readily and honestly when I'm behind the wheel. If, for example, I get offended easily at the mistakes of other drivers, I'm probably getting offended at coworkers or family members more often than I'd like to think. If I'm completely self-absorbed in my mission to get to a certain place at a certain time, that usually translates into an overall self-absorption in what I'm trying to accomplish in that particular season of life. Whatever I've stuffed in real relationships comes out in my "relationships" with other cars. My temperament on the highway is a snapshot of the bigger picture, a diagnostic tool with startling accuracy.

Knowing that has helped me see the source of much of the weightiness that I and others carry around. We'd like to think that our burdens are primarily about people and circumstances, but our own attitudes and perspectives are a big part of the problem. On the highway, for example, what would happen if I just decided to let people cut in front of me? if I backed off and added some space between my front bumper and the other car's back bumper? if I looked for opportunities to let others go first? What would I have to lose? A few seconds of my day? I'd gladly trade a few seconds for a peaceful heart. But for some reason, that's a hard attitude to implement—especially when the context is the big issues of life and not a morning commute.

I want most of this book to focus on the solutions to our burdensome lives, not on the problem itself. And we're getting there. But before we dive deeper into the answers, we need to spend another chapter looking at our burdens. Somehow just seeing where they come from helps to lighten them, or at least prepares us to deal with them appropriately. When we're able to identify them, their power begins to dissipate.

Heavy Weights

Many of our burdens come from our misperceptions and distorted thinking—we'll look at those in a bit—but some of them simply come during the normal course of life. We can be entirely in the will of God in our outward circumstances and inner desires yet still be burdened about the issues we have to deal with. Even with a clean conscience, we can have major stresses.

Decisions and direction

Professionals who study consumer behavior talk about the problem of "overchoice," but it really applies to every area of life. Never in the history of the world have we had as many choices as we have now. "Offering more choices by itself seems like a positive development," says the Wikipedia entry on overchoice. "In fact, however, it hides an underlying problem: faced with too many choices, consumers have trouble making optimal satisfying choices, and thus as a result can be indecisive, unhappy, and even refrain from making the choice (purchase) at all."[1]

Of course, the problem of making a decision is nothing new. When faced with a variety of options, we can rule many out right away, but others seem good. We are starved for direction from God. We want a peek into the future, an exhaustive and infallible list of pros and cons, or some supernatural guidance that will just tell us what to do. That's why horoscopes are so appealing to so many people. They claim to offer inside information on what's coming down the road. We crave that kind of advantage when we have to make a decision. We look for anything that will take some of the pressure off.

The responsibility of making decisions can be oppressive. We can't escape the need to decide. Life is full of choices; even choosing not to make them is a choice. An awareness that minor decisions today may have major repercussions tomorrow—it takes a small rudder to determine the direction of an entire ship—only adds to the weight. That weight can really stress us out.

Responsibilities and workload

Is there any way around this? Certain seasons of life seem heavy with extra responsibilities. That's normal. The problem is when seasons expand into years or even decades. Some careers or family roles can be overwhelming in their demands. A forty-hour-a-week job can easily turn into a fifty- or sixty-hour obligation, and family members can require long periods of intense attention or long-term care. Most Christians have a strong desire to be faithful in all of their duties. But duties that become a drain on time, energy, or resources create a lot of worries.

This is especially true when you are responsible for the welfare of other people. It's sobering to know that your decisions at work can eventually determine whether a number of people will be able to keep their jobs, their health insurance, and their houses. Some people are able to make decisions about layoffs and firings easily; others get ulcers about such decisions. In an interdependent society in which each person affects many others, our choices can be an overwhelming responsibility.

Finances

We live in the wealthiest era in history, and most people reading this book are from a society with the highest standard of living in this era. That puts us in the most economically advantageous position human beings have ever experienced—and still hardly anyone thinks they have enough money. Our incomes aren't quite large enough, our budgets are always a little too tight, and in spite of all of our assets, most of us carry some kind of debt. On top of that, we worry about our financial security in the future.

This is a strange phenomenon. It seems the more we acquire, the more concerned we are about maintaining it. The more diverse our personal economies are, the more scattered our thoughts are about them. The more opportunities we have to invest or spend, the more decisions we need to make. Those who have relatively little are preoccupied with financial issues; and those with obscenely large bank accounts are preoccupied with financial issues. Few people have learned how to deal with their money without stress.

Health

Half an hour before I began writing this section, several of us at the office got news that one of our coworkers was just diagnosed with stage-three cancer. One of our colleagues died a couple of years ago from the same kind of cancer. Both were relatively young women—and completely surprised—when they came face-to-face with the frightening news of their condition. Neither had any reason to suspect that she would be hit with a dreaded disease.

Most of us are aware that even robust health can be taken away from us at a moment's notice. Some of us actually spend time worrying about that possibility. But even if we aren't concerned with life-threatening illness for ourselves, we're concerned about it for someone. We all have family members, friends, and/or coworkers who have had to battle with an out-of-the-blue injury or illness. It's a lingering threat in the back of our minds that can weigh us down.

Relationships

There's virtually no end to the ways we can worry about relationships. When we're single, we spend a lot of energy thinking about finding the right person to marry. When we're married, we spend a lot of energy thinking about how to improve our marriage or even hold on to it. If we have children, we worry about their welfare. We may worry about finding friends, relating to them, impressing them, not offending them, and more. We stress about conflict and how to resolve it—or if a relationship is already broken, how it can be healed or whether it even should be. Negative themes woven in and out of many of our relationships can include mistrust, blame, guilt, boredom, and insensitivity. Relationships can be the most complicating aspect of our lives.

Heavier Weights

Another category of burdens involves the stresses we inflict on ourselves, usually unintentionally. These come from having an unbalanced perspective, having dysfunctional patterns of thought and behavior, or focusing on the wrong issues. Nearly everyone encounters some of these at some point in life, but none of them are necessary. Unlike the stresses above—decisions, responsibilities, finances, health, and relationships—these aren't inevitable. Even so, nearly all of us are affected by the following burdens in degrees ranging from very minor to all-consuming.

Materialism, wealth, and a comfortable lifestyle

Striving for a certain lifestyle can be stressful. There's nothing wrong with wanting to live in a certain way, but the drive to get there often becomes much more important to us than it should. The American dream can be a terrible burden to bear—and, at certain seasons in life, very difficult to maintain. We have a vision for the kind of home we want to live in, the things we want to be able to do and buy, and all the trappings that come along with that picture. And we often just assume that this is a realistic vision and that anything that falls short of it is failure. There's a lot of pressure involved in accomplishing that goal, and there's even more involved in maintaining it. A lot of people are outwardly living the life they envisioned but being drained of all their energy by the rat race necessary to maintain the lifestyle. There's no joy in that way of life.

It's amazing how absurdly we behave sometimes without even realizing how senseless we look. In a consumer society, we are constantly acquiring more. Then the size of our homes has to catch up with the amount of stuff we have; we need bigger places. And if we acquired our stuff with credit, our incomes have to catch up with the amount of stuff we have too; we need more money. So we work harder in order to expand our incomes, our properties, and our possessions—and then feel the weight of an overextended lifestyle.

The storage-unit phenomenon is a visible symptom of this dynamic. I know there are plenty of valid reasons for renting storage units from time to time because I've done it myself. But I read somewhere that most units are rented for an average of eighteen months, at the end of which time most renters decide to sell all their stuff anyway. In other words, we pay far more than our possessions are worth just to house them, and when we finally figure out the absurdity of that situation—thousands of dollars later—we get rid of our things, just as we could have done in the first place. Meanwhile, we carry a lot of mental stress just by having more than we need.

Pride, self-promotion, reputation, and image

One of the most tragically humorous characters in the Bible is Haman, the villain in the book of Esther. Completely self-absorbed and obsessed about his own status, he could have enjoyed all the benefits of his position in the king's court. Instead, he had to tirelessly promote himself and couldn't even enjoy a banquet for long because he was eaten up with bitterness toward a rival. His pride drove him to seek fulfillment in his own glory, but prohibited him from enjoying even a taste of the glory he sought.

Few of us are infected with that degree of pride, but many of us are overly concerned with our own images and reputations. If you've done even a little bit of image management for yourself, you know how exhausting it can be. It makes you feel like the Wizard of Oz—pulling levers and pushing buttons as fast as you can, desperately hoping no one pulls the curtain back to expose the real you. Sure, it might be stressful to let people see us as we really are. But it's a much bigger burden to cover up our flaws.

Pride in any form is a high-maintenance attitude. It forces us to do things to impress people, tell half-truths or even outright lies to build ourselves up or tear someone else down, accomplish things that don't really interest us but look good to others, buy things we can't afford in order to convey a certain image, accept jobs for the status they carry rather than the actual mission they fulfill, and so on. We may not think of humility as a fulfilling virtue, but it's easy to maintain and much better than the alternative. Pride can make us downright miserable.

Agendas and expectations

Everyone has dreams, goals, and plans. But if they aren't God-given dreams, goals, and plans, they can consume our lives and eat away at our sense of satisfaction. It has been said that an expectation is a "predetermined resentment," and there's some truth in that. Not all expectations set us up for resentment, but a lot of them do. When we, other people, or circumstances don't meet them, we get very frustrated. We try to pressure people to cooperate and force situations to work out the way we want. The desire to control and manipulate greatly complicates our relationships and causes us to feel very weighed down. Staying "on top" of things is a dizzying lifestyle.

Most of us have known people (or *been* people) who have such a strong agenda for their lives and the people around them that they can't help but be miserable. It's a heavy burden to expect so much and, inevitably, be disappointed by all the ways life doesn't work out as expected. A strong agenda is an asset when it's a God-given mission—and even then, only when we trust God to fulfill that mission—but it's a heavy liability when it's an inflexible personal ambition. It's bound to feel futile eventually.

Judgments, criticisms, and offenses

A well-known professional basketball player recently got into some verbal sparring with a former coach through the media. In one of his comments to an interviewer, the player said very emphatically that he "demanded" respect because of his long and storied career. Aside from the obvious fact that you can't demand respect from others—they either give it to you or they don't—the cocky player was venting a common sentiment that most of us let simmer beneath the surface. We have a nearly endless capacity to nurture offenses and grudges.

Think of the variety of ways we do this. Someone ahead of us in line at the grocery store has unloaded her cart when she suddenly remembers she forgot to pick up a gallon of milk. She casually asks the bagger to run and get her one and doesn't even hint at an apologetic glance in our direction. Though that means we will have to wait an additional two minutes to begin unloading our purchases, it really doesn't have any other effect at all—other than offending us. Someone forgets to acknowledge a contribution we've made at work or at church, and though it doesn't actually cause anyone to think less of us, the apparent lack of appreciation really gets under our skin. Someone questions a decision we made, and immediately we get defensive—as though that person's lack of support makes any difference as to whether we are right or wrong. And we don't just get defensive, we go on the offense pretty frequently, making snap judgments about other people and mentally putting them down. The point is that many of us seem to have an unspoken, internal competition between ourselves and everyone around us.

Urgency and busyness

Back in 1967, Charles Hummel wrote about "The Tyranny of the Urgent" in a booklet for InterVarsity Press, and it seems that our increasing pace of life has only intensified the problem. Technology has made communication easier, but "easy" doesn't help when you're trying to create margin in your life. It only increases the speed of the demands placed on us. We're busier than ever.

Hummel pointed out that our time-crunch problems are usually a matter of having misplaced priorities. We sacrifice the things that are important for whatever is urgent. The result is a very stressful schedule dictated by the demands of the moment. We think our schedules are full of necessary activities and obligations, but that's only because of our definition of "necessary." We are almost always busier than God intends for us to be.

Most of us want more hours in the day, but I have a hunch that even if we got them, they would fill up with the same kinds of activities that already weigh us down, and we still wouldn't have enough time. The answer to feeling overextended isn't spreading our overextension into a longer day. It's in developing the right priorities in the time we have.

Fear of loss or misfortune

Most of us can find things to worry about if we try. A hint of a symptom might cause us to imagine all the dire illnesses that could be stirring within us. A single financial setback can stimulate all sorts of thinking about how we would manage a major financial crisis. Hearing about someone else's accident almost begs us to think of how the same thing could happen to us. We have a tendency to turn molehill difficulties into mountains of crisis long before anything actually happens to us.

Regrets

We all have things in our pasts we would do differently if we got another chance. Some of those can turn into huge regrets—decisions that we know have dramatically

> We have a tendency to turn molehill difficulties into mountains of crisis long before anything actually happens to us.

and negatively altered the course of our lives. Seeing the damage we've caused makes us wish we could turn back time. We wonder what life would be like if we hadn't done the things we did. Regrets are heavy loads to bear.

Sin, addictions, and guilt

The wages of sin may be death, but it demands an even greater payment than that. Sin always has consequences that complicate our lives, especially when it involves a habitual dependence that can be expensive, time-consuming, or damaging to our health. Beyond the outward consequences of sin is one devilish burden that can outweigh all others: guilt. When we're carrying a sense of guilt around, every other area of life can seem overwhelmingly heavy. If we want to live an unburdened life, we have to understand and apply the solution to our sin and guilt.

Unfortunately, the weight of guilt is just as painful when the guilt is false. The sense of shame many people carry within them because of some past abuse or trauma is as crippling as the real thing, even though the bearer didn't do anything wrong. The remedy for false guilt is different than the remedy for true guilt—you don't need to confess and repent for being abused or having shattered self-esteem—but the need to deal with it is just as great. It's impossible to live with a sense of weightlessness while holding on to shame.

> The wages of sin may be death, but it demands an even greater payment than that.

Souls Stretched Thin

Jesus told twin parables about people giving up all they had in order to gain something of much greater value. One was a man who found a treasure hidden in a field. With joy, he went and sold all that he had and bought the field. The other was a merchant who discovered an extremely valuable pearl. He, too, sold all he had and bought the pearl.[2] These parables describe the exchange we make in order to come into God's Kingdom; we have to be willing to lose everything in order to gain Christ. But they also describe a by-product of coming into his Kingdom—the unburdened life. God gives us an amazing offer: we can trade all of our complications for his peace, all of our stresses for his strength, all of our neediness for his supply. We turn over our burdens to him, and he takes them. What we receive in return is himself.

That's a no-brainer of an exchange. We'll talk more about what it entails and how we actually apply it to real life, but the point is that we have a choice to make. On one hand, we can continue to worry about things we can't control, be driven by petty slights or overinflated agendas, get irritated by people we don't want to deal with, or be burdened by work we don't want to do. On the other hand, we can relinquish the key to our lives to someone much more capable of managing them. Sure, we'll have to radically submit to his plan, but considering how well our own plans work for us, that shouldn't be a hard decision to make. Transferring the weight that holds us down to someone much stronger is a real, viable option.

When we do that decisively—and it really does require a forceful, resolute decision—we exchange our scattered interests for one overriding passion. The problem is that we have diversified souls. We're jugglers trying to manage life and treat a multitude of symptoms, some of which we hardly even know are there. Like the man who found a treasure in a field and the merchant who found a valuable pearl, we can trade in multiple concerns for a single one. When we learn how to focus our diversified souls on one master, we find our burdens a lot less weighty.

The "After" Picture

Infomercials for weight-loss plans invariably show a multitude of before and after pictures to demonstrate the effectiveness of the program. In other words, they show you pictures of the promise. In a sense, the Bible does the same thing. It tells us what kind of people we can be when we surrender our burdens to God. It also tells us God's solution and shows us his promises for each of the burdens in our lives.

Our problem is that we have diversified souls.

We can see this if we go through the same categories of burdens listed above and apply biblical truth to them. What we'll find in virtually every case is that our worries are lying to us. They directly contradict biblical promises and principles.

Decisions and direction

Is there any shortage in the Bible of promises assuring us that God will guide us if we let him? If we look to him and not to our own understanding, he'll lead us wherever he wants us to go.[3] His sheep hear his voice.[4] Even when we aren't sure of the direction we're going, we're told that he will determine our steps.[5] The question isn't whether God will give us direction; it's whether we believe that he is when he's doing it. His desire is to lead us into his purposes.

Responsibilities and workload

God built at least one solution for this into his plan: the Sabbath. It's a never-revoked command—a "permanent" law[6]—that he himself modeled for us at Creation. Most people think they are too busy to take a Sabbath rest, much like we often think we don't have enough money to give a regular offering to God. But in God's economy, taking time off (and giving a portion of one's income) generally makes life more efficient. And for those responsibilities that aren't addressed by a once-a-week rest, God offers his strength to help us carry them. His desire is for us to be empowered by him in all we do.

Finances

Jesus told us not to worry about the necessities of life, and Paul assured the Philippians that God would provide all their needs according to his riches.[7] There's no need to spiritualize this promise. Though it certainly applies to the range of human need, including spiritual needs, the context of Paul's statement was finances. God's desire is for us to trust him and expect his provision.

Health

God calls himself our Healer,[8] and Jesus spent quite a bit of his ministry healing people. So did the apostles. I've seen God do dramatic miracles of healing in our day too. I can't explain why he doesn't in every case, but I'm convinced he wants us to seek him for healing in any situation in which we need it. His Word invites us—practically pleads with us—to come to him in faith when we're sick and hurting. His desire is for us to depend on him physically as well as spiritually.

Relationships

God is relational at his core, from the fellowship of the Trinity to his enormous love for the world. Jesus came to reconcile us to God, and he gave us a ministry of reconciliation. His Spirit strengthens us in his love. The two greatest commandments are meant to establish our relationships with God and with each other. From Genesis 1 to Revelation 22, God is concerned with the quality of relationships. His desire is to help us establish them, strengthen them, and heal the ones that need healing. We can count on him to do that.

Materialism, wealth, and a comfortable lifestyle

The reason we have a hard time trusting God for our well-being is that "hard master" syndrome we discussed in the last chapter. We know he'll provide for our needs, but is he generous? Does he ever give us our wants? Or do we have to go after those on our own? The testimony of Scripture is that God gives good gifts[9] and blesses people like Abraham, David, Solomon, and quite a few other people with wealth and other pleasures and comforts. That doesn't mean wealth is an inherent part of the gospel, but it does prove that God isn't stingy. His desire is for us to trust him to give us exactly what he wants to give us. That's often much more than we think.

Pride, self-promotion, reputation, and image

Throughout Scripture, God defends the humble but opposes the proud.[10] For some reason, many of us have a deep-seated drive to elevate ourselves. The fundamental problem is that we don't trust him to support us. What we don't realize is that this drive directly opposes the way God wants to work with us. Our regard for our own images and status brings us into conflict with him, but he provides ample strength and status to those who humbly depend on him.[11] In other words, the way up in the Kingdom of God is to go down. God's desire is for us to live completely unassuming, unpretentious lives and let him lift us up whenever and however he wants.

Agendas and expectations

God makes it clear that he has plans and purposes for our lives. When we live willfully, focused on our own agendas and fixed on rigid expectations, we're directing ourselves rather than letting him direct us. The fundamental problem is that we don't trust God to accomplish his will—or that we don't trust that his will is better than our own will. When we find ourselves taking matters into our own hands, we're revealing a lack of confidence in his ability or willingness to accomplish his good purposes for us. But his desire is for us to trust him to be in the driver's seat of our lives.

Judgments, criticisms, and offenses

If we had the humility and trust we are supposed to have, we'd have no need to criticize others or to be offended when we feel slighted. When we have a strong competitive reaction to those around us, we're revealing a deep insecurity about our position in God's Kingdom. Our fundamental problem is a lack of trust that he will defend us and establish us in the roles he wants us to have. But as children of God and heirs of his Kingdom, we don't need to have a sense of rivalry with anyone. His desire is for us to relax, enjoy his favor, and trust him to defend us and position us where he wants to.

Urgency and busyness

Jesus never seemed to be in a hurry, even when one of his closest friends was at the point of death and needed him.[12] Yet somehow he was able to accomplish more in three years than anyone else has ever accomplished in a lifetime. Why? Because he allowed God to direct his schedule. We can do that too. We may deal with the reality of nine-to-five jobs and calendar appointments, but we can still live without a sense of urgency. The reason we don't is that we rarely trust that God is sovereignly guiding us. We often don't recognize the "divine appointments" he sets up for us, and we often wouldn't be able to respond to them even if we did recognize them because our schedules are so filled with unnecessary clutter. God's desire is for us to have enough margin in our lives that we can go wherever he leads at any time.

Fear of loss or misfortune

God is the gatekeeper of our lives. In the context of our faith in him, we can't gain anything he doesn't provide, and we can't lose anything he doesn't allow us to lose. Even Job, who suffered unusual loss, acknowledged that the Lord gives and he takes away.[13] Though few of us are likely to ever experience Job's degree of loss, we still fear misfortune. And the Bible never guarantees us that we won't have Job-like experiences. But it does guarantee that we can trust God in every twist and turn of our lives. We can never experience any kind of loss that he does not have some kind of provision for. Our problem is worrying that we might experience hardship without finding his grace sufficient. That's a lack of trust in his provision. His desire is for us to be able to handle any event with the clear confidence that he is present with us and helping us through it.

Regrets

We don't really understand how Romans 8:28 works— how God works everything together for the good of those who love him. But that verse applies even to our own bad choices. Joseph applied

We can never experience any kind of loss that God does not have some kind of provision for.

this principle to the evil betrayal of his brothers. They meant to do harm, but God used it for good.[14] We're tempted in our regrets to nurture a sense of bitterness, and it's easy to do. That's because we don't see God's hand in every event, and we don't really trust his ability to work all things for our good. We live with a sneaking suspicion that we'll get his consolation prizes in life, not his best gifts. His desire is for us to be able to live with complete confidence in his ability to redeem everything in our pasts.

Sin, addictions, and guilt

God's solution for these burdens is well known by anyone with even a basic familiarity with the gospel. But how easily does it sink in? The truth of our complete forgiveness and the complete removal of guilt and shame is hard to fully embrace. Many of us suspect that what we've done is too bad, or that we've done it for too long, for God to really give us a clean slate. We know his mercy as an objective fact but not as a personal experience. We often don't live as though we deeply know it. We don't allow it to heal all of our emotional wounds and scars. But God wants us to experience his power over sin—not just the truth of our forgiveness, but God's removal of all of its effects in our lives. Our problem is a lack of trust that sin's power is fully broken. Even after we've been Christians for years, we still tend to talk about the power of the old nature more than his power to overcome it. But if the Son sets you free, you will be thoroughly free.[15] God's desire is for us to experience real freedom in the depths of our souls.

The Common Denominator

Do you see a common thread running throughout these burdens? The key variable when we don't experience freedom from them is a lack of trust. Whenever we feel the weight of our burdens, there's some aspect of God's character or some truth from his Word that we aren't fully trusting. That's the area of our lives we need to focus on if we're ever going to feel free. In order to go through life with the lightness God wants us to have, we have to actually believe what he has told us.

We'll try to get to the root of our mistrust in the next chapter because we can't go any further toward getting rid of our worries until we do. That forceful, resolute decision to let go of the things that weigh us down can't be made in a vacuum. In order for it to stick we have to make it in complete confidence that God is there to handle the things we're letting go of. Deep down inside, we need to be able to rely on him to meet us at every point of need.

CHAPTER 4

TRUST

JESUS AND THE disciples were in a boat on the Sea of Galilee—that seemed to be one of Jesus' preferred settings for teaching them lessons about faith—and a storm came up. A *fierce* storm, actually. It was violent enough that high waves crashed over the bow and filled the boat with water. Strong winds blew, the vessel bounced up and down on the waves, and in a startlingly absurd picture, one of the passengers slept on a cushion in the back. Jesus was apparently oblivious to the savage forces of nature.

Galilean fishing boats weren't big. They didn't have insulated cabins to block out the elements. In fact, they didn't have cabins at all. Jesus would have been unable to avoid feeling the wind and the water, he would have heard the shouts of his friends, and he would have bounced on the waves as relentlessly as everyone else did. And somehow he slept.

Jesus' complete disregard for the danger his friends faced bothered them. He wasn't buying into their worry. In fact, he wasn't even aware of it. It's amazing that they had to wake him, but they did—frantically. And when he sat up, they hurled an accusation at him: "Don't you care that we're going to drown?"[1] Yes, this was the same Master who had spoken kind words and shown enormous compassion to them and others. Of course he cared. But he looked like he didn't. That made no sense. So they asked.

Calmly, Jesus got up and answered their question without actually answering it. He rebuked the raging elements, watched them calm down, and then turned to his panicky friends: "Why are you afraid? Do you still have no faith?"[2] These are pointed questions, and we know that if we were in the disciples' situation, these questions would be pointed at us too. And who could blame us? Would anyone in his or her right mind assume everything is fine when a storm is about to sink a small boat and the one person who could offer help is asleep? It's hard to imagine anyone joining Jesus in his nap in that situation. But that's exactly what he expected them to be able to do—or at least the kind of attitude he wanted them to have.

In our own storms, most of us ask the same slanderous question the disciples asked. We aren't always aware of it, but we really wrestle in our crises with whether Jesus actually cares that we're drowning. And until we settle that question, it's impossible to live an unburdened life. As long as there's some doubt lingering in our minds about whether God will take care of us, we'll bear the weight of our problems. We can't cast our cares on the Lord—not completely—until we're able to trust him completely.

It would be nearly impossible to overstate the warfare we will face on this point. Trust is an epic battle in the minds of most believers. It's a brutal battle that goes way back to the first temptation, that disaster in the Garden that introduced us to all of our burdens in the first place. The world and the enemy seem to conspire relentlessly to create fears, doubts, and mistrust in our minds. If we are ever going to get to a place of trusting God—the kind of trust that allows us to experience deep-rooted peace—then we will have to contend for it. We will have to learn to vehemently resist any suggestion that God won't come through for us. We will have to fight in order to rest.

> **We will have to fight in order to rest.**

An Ability to Sleep

Family dysfunction doesn't get much worse than this. One of the king's sons had raped his half sister, and the king didn't do anything about it. So the half sister's full brother took revenge by killing the offender, and a long-standing feud broke out within the family. When the vengeful son eventually gathered enough support to stage a coup against his father, the king and his men vacated the capital to avoid a heated battle and potential massacre in the city. The king fled in hopes that God would see fit to bring him back under less hostile circumstances.

Those are the conditions under which David wrote Psalm 3. He had fled Jerusalem to avoid confrontation with Absalom and his numerous troops. David the king was hanging on to power by a thread. David the father had already lost one son to vengeance, and he had been estranged from this one for a number of years. Now Absalom had become aggressive. He planned an attack on David's men and openly slept with the women in David's harem as a statement of his intent to usurp the throne. It's hard to imagine a more stressful time.

David didn't cover up his burdens or deny they existed. He acknowledged in the first two verses of the psalm that his enemies were numerous and many were predicting his downfall: "O Lord, I have so many enemies; so many are against me. So many are saying, 'God will never rescue him!'" And for all David knew, his foes might be right. His past was stained with his sin with Bathsheba and his violence against enemies, and his own son had turned against him. That was enough potential evidence of God's disfavor for David to allow a relative of Saul to hurl curses and stones at him as he left Jerusalem. David wondered if the curses were legitimate. He didn't have an entirely clean conscience.

Even so, he knew God. In spite of his own shortcomings,

his seemingly crumbling kingdom, his to-the-death family feud, and his tolerance of curses aimed directly at him, David cried out to God and trusted God to answer. "You, O LORD, are a shield around me; you are my glory, the one who holds my head high. . . . I lay down and slept, yet I woke up in safety, for the LORD was watching over me. I am not afraid of ten thousand enemies who surround me on every side."[3]

It takes a lot of trust to be able to rest peacefully in the midst of such tumultuous events. We know from hints in the story of this episode in David's life that he didn't walk through it in complete confidence from beginning to end.[4] He experienced deep grief and legitimate fears. But somehow he was able to shift his attitude from fear to trust and from sadness to hope. By the end of the psalm, he was declaring victory in the name of the Lord. He eventually faced a painfully uncertain, life-or-death situation with faith.

God didn't take David's burdens away—at least not in the sense of removing adverse circumstances or stripping David of his responsibilities. He did, however, give David strength and confidence that

Instead of removing our need to trust, God teaches us how to trust.

he was working in the situation and bearing the weight of them on his infinite shoulders. He does the same with us. Instead of removing our need to trust, he teaches us how to trust. The need remains, but our dependence on him grows stronger. And, in the process, our loads become lighter.

Trust doesn't come easily for anyone other than children, which is perhaps why Jesus told us to have the faith of a child. Most of us have developed some level of mistrust in God from past experiences, particularly those times when God either felt absent or perhaps even seemed to be working against us. One of my pastors refers to one such event as "the elephant in the room of her soul"—a big, lingering question about where God was during a crisis moment in her childhood. We all have these doubts at some point in our lives about whether God is really on our side. All of us have gone through trials and crises that left us wondering why God didn't intervene. Where was he? Why didn't he answer that huge, desperate prayer? Why did he let that tragedy happen? The lack of answers to these questions nags at us, undermining our trust in the one who tells us he is trustworthy.

There isn't an easy solution for getting this deep-seated mistrust out of our hearts—if by "easy" we mean "effortless." But the solution begins with a simple approach: we decide to trust God regardless of how things look or how little we understand him. Ever since the Fall, the world, the flesh, and the devil seem constantly to be conspiring to convince us that God is not good, that he can't be trusted. And listening to those voices or judging by appearances isn't going to resolve that false perception for us. We have to choose to believe what God says about himself and what we know to be true from the ways he *has* worked in our lives. No matter how things look, no matter how inexplicable certain life experiences seem to be, he isn't a hard master. Insisting on that truth is a matter of living by faith rather than by sight, and it can be extremely difficult. We need divine help with it and lots of encouragement to fuel us. Whatever it takes, we can't let our faith submit to the dictates of our experiences. Those who persist in the stubborn belief that God is good eventually find that their experiences have to bow to their faith.

Trust is a vital aspect of our relationship with God. The Bible explicitly urges us well over a hundred times to trust God and implicitly teaches us to do so even more often. In the Psalms alone, trust in God is mentioned over fifty times. We often read of David or another psalmist declaring trust in the Lord and remember only their statements of faith. But the Psalms are a virtual field manual on how to move from an attitude of fear, anxiety, and stress to an attitude of trust and rest. These writings are more than historical information. They are case studies. They show us how to cultivate this essential approach to life.

We've seen how the weighed-down feelings we have can usually be traced back to some underlying mistrust of God. And we've seen a lot of the ways we can talk ourselves out of trusting him by wondering if there's legal fine print underneath his promises or assuming that his promises don't apply to our specific situations. But the solution has to be more than a simple "trust God." It begins there, but it has to be fueled by more than human willpower. We know we need to trust him, but until we're convinced that it will make a genuine difference in our lives and that God will come through for us, it doesn't help much for someone to tell us to trust him. We first have to know the benefits of trusting him.

Why Trust?

Perhaps we've heard the instruction to trust God so often that we've become numb to its implications, but it's more than an encouraging pat on the back. Though telling ourselves to trust him may feel like a mood-boosting platitude, it's the first step in a profound change in perspective. It literally can change the quality of our lives.

Look at it this way: we're always trusting in something. Some people choose to trust in impersonal natural processes as the overriding mechanism of how life works. Some people chalk everything up to random chance. Some place a lot of faith in their own intellects or abilities, or in the intellects and abilities of people they look up to. Most of us trust history to some degree, assuming that however things have gone in the past is an indicator of how they will go in the future. And considering how many of us have experienced negative circumstances and how often we've been disappointed, the deck is stacked against us when we try to trust God and have faith. We may even end up trusting in the tendency for things to go wrong more than we trust in God's willingness to protect, provide, and deliver. But regardless of our focus, at every moment in our lives, we are trusting something or someone.

So the gist of the scriptural command isn't "trust God instead of not trusting him." It's "trust God instead of trusting everything else you invest your beliefs in." In any situation in life, that's imperative. We have an opportunity in virtually every circumstance to make a statement of faith. And if we want to live with a sense of freedom, we absolutely have to shift our trust from lesser gods to the one true God.

We have plenty of incentive to do so. According to the Psalms, we can say that God has never abandoned or forsaken anyone who trusted him and sought him[5] and that no one who has trusted him has ever been disappointed.[6] Those who trust him will never be shamed or disgraced,[7] nor will they ever lack any good thing.[8] Our trust in him eliminates the need for fear,[9] and all the power is somehow taken out of any bad news we might receive.[10] In fact, we can know that we will never be defeated in any real sense of the word but will rather endure forever.[11]

One of the Psalms gives us a picture of God storing up his goodness—literally hoarding it or saving it up like treasure—in order to bless those who take refuge in him.[12] Another assures us that his unfailing, relentless love surrounds—completely envelops—those who trust him.[13] Everyone who trusts him will

- be freely pardoned;[14]
- be rescued;[15]
- go into their land of promise and possess it;[16]
- live in the land in safety and under his blessing;[17]

- be happy and blessed;[18]
- have ample reason to praise him;[19]
- thrive like an olive tree.[20]

God helps those who trust him,[21] he gives food to those who trust him,[22] and he is a shield of protection to those who trust him.[23] Trust in God inevitably results in joy.[24]

Do you understand what this means? The Psalms are giving us a portrait of someone who trusts in God: happy, fearless, full of joy, worshipful, free, well provided for, overflowing with good gifts, protected, safe, secure, victorious, and thriving. Apparently, God responds to our heartfelt trust by pouring out his goodness on us. One gets the impression from Scripture that the thought of a trusting soul not receiving food or protection or blessing ought to be absolutely inconceivable. It would make no sense for a loving father to observe the earnest trust of a dependent child and not respond to it with an outpouring of love. If Scripture is even remotely true, God honors our trust. He always lives up to it. We open our mouths in trust, and he fills them.

Anyone who believes that God inspired the words of Scripture and that his promises in the Bible are true can't help but be encouraged and strengthened by the clearly stated benefits of trusting God. In fact, it may help to read through those benefits again and again, slowly and thoughtfully, letting them sink in. Look up the specific verses cited above and even read them out loud. Rehearsing the truth like that makes a powerful statement to our minds and goes a long way toward undoing the lies we've believed. If we can integrate these truths into our way of thinking, our burdens will begin to feel lighter.

"Yes, But . . ."

I've noticed a strange phenomenon in mainstream evangelical Christianity. I call it "yes-but theology." In our well-meaning attempts to prevent people from misunderstanding the Bible, we focus much of our teachings on all the possible abuses and false interpretations of a verse or passage. Then we draw narrow lines around the text so people will learn precisely what the verse or passage intended to say. But in doing so, we often draw the limits too tightly or too rigidly; or we draw the limits perfectly accurately but then focus entirely on the limits rather than what's inside them. The result is that with any truth or principle that seems too good to be true, we say "yes, but . . ." and then explain why it doesn't mean what it looks like it means.[25]

Take, for example, the passage in which Jesus told his disciples, "Whatever you ask for in prayer, believe that you have received it, and it will be yours."[26] I've heard sermons on that verse in which 90 percent of the teaching is about what it doesn't mean. It isn't giving us permission to "name it and claim it"; it doesn't mean we can just ask for selfish desires; there are a lot of conditions to prayer; we have to ask according to God's will; and so on. And while all of that is true, by the time the sermon gets to what the verse *does* mean, Jesus' words have pretty much lost all the power they had in their original form. There's nothing inspiring left in this promise. Its truth means practically nothing when it's surrounded by theological barbed-wire fences saying, "Don't get too close to this one."

For some reason, Jesus uttered this statement in bare-naked form. He just put it out there for the disciples without any noticeable caveats around it. He did what we're afraid to do: state a bold truth and let people embrace it and perhaps even misunderstand it. Why did he do that without warning against its abuses? I believe it's because of the way we fallen creatures perceive the world. We question good news readily and accept it reluctantly. In order for us to have a balanced view of his truth, he has to emphasize the extravagance of it. We are skeptics by nature. We don't need help thinking of reasons the good news isn't all that good. We need help believing it.

We have a mind-numbing capacity for making simple theological truths complex.

The same dynamic works for all those verses that tell us not to worry, that God bears our burdens, that we can trust him, and that we're free. Our natural reaction to them is "yes, but . . ." followed by multifaceted explanations of all the possible exceptions. We have a mind-numbing capacity for making simple theological truths complex, and it usually shows up when we're interpreting Scripture through painful real-life experience.

That's understandable. I know, for example, the thoughts that can come to mind when we read through the benefits of trusting God. We can think of people who don't fit the description—people who trusted God and still died of cancer or remained unemployed for a year or two. I can imagine John the Baptist sitting in prison with Psalm 50:15 on his lips: "Call on me when you are in trouble, and I will rescue you, and you will give me glory." I have no doubt that John trusted God, yet he was executed anyway. And I don't think situations like that require us to redefine "rescue" or "healing" or anything else we normally redefine when we wrestle with a promise. There are times when God chooses, for very good reasons, not to do what he indicated he would do as a general rule.

The problem is that the exceptions loom much larger in our own minds than the fulfillments do. Most of us say "yes, but" much more easily than we say "thank you, Lord."[27] Somehow we have to reverse that tendency and assume that, in most cases, God will do for us exactly as he said he would do. And we have to refuse to worry about the possibility that he might not.

I can't explain the exceptional cases that cause us to question God's assurances. Maybe there are times when God chooses not to act because the person in question really didn't trust God, or maybe the hardship he or she went through was actually a means to something much greater or part of a much bigger plan for which, in the eternal scheme of things, God rewards his participants amply. I do know, however, that even in hard situations, God never violates our trust in him. He never proves untrustworthy. He doesn't tease us with false promises. If we're told so emphatically that we can trust him, there's a very good reason we can. He means for us to read his Word and be filled with confidence that he will behave in a way that is consistent with his character and true to his promises.

He also means for us to trust him *before* we see how the situation plays out. If we're waiting to see what God is going to do in our circumstances before we trust him, that isn't trust. That's why we're told that faith is the evidence of things *not seen*,[28] that we should fix our eyes on what is invisible,[29] and that we walk by faith and not by sight.[30] Whether we're looking ahead to eternal realities or trusting God day to day, we have to learn to rely on spiritual senses and not on what our eyes see and our ears hear. We have to be able to rely on God in the midst of our crises. He generally waits until we trust him before he shows how trustworthy he is. In the meantime, he gives us his Word and tells us to hang on to it without fear.

I'm determined not to live with a yes-but belief system. When my experience and a particular promise don't line up, I want to look at my experience through the lens of the promise rather than looking at the promise through the lens of my experience. I want to bring my understanding up to the level of God's truth, not bring his truth down to the level of my understanding. I want to accept the extravagance of his Word without focusing on all the exceptions I can't explain.

That's the only way I know how to live by faith according to the words he has spoken. And I believe this is the only way we can live in the freedom he wants us to have.

Deep and Deeper

Caveats aside, the Bible overwhelmingly affirms the joy of those who choose to put their trust in God whether trust makes sense to them or not. "They are abundantly satisfied with the fullness of Your house, and You give them drink from the river of Your pleasures."[31] Verses like this gush with unrestrained goodwill.

Why, then, are so many Christians still not "abundantly satisfied"? Because reading or hearing affirmations like this isn't enough. Neither is nodding our heads when we read or hear them. We have to make a specific choice to believe them and contend for that choice against all other voices. Sometimes this is a brutal war; it seems that the forces of hell are determined to knock us out of our trust in God. Considering how trust was a key battlefield in Eden, that only makes sense. The first temptation was an attempt to impugn God's goodness, and that basic accusation against him whispers to us relent-

> **Relying on God is not a passive attitude.**

lessly throughout our lives. But we have to contend anyway. Relying on God is not a passive attitude. Restful, perhaps, but never passive.

There are different kinds of trust in God:

Everyday trust. For starters, we trust in him as a general attitude in normal, everyday life. Regardless of how circumstances look, how our moods fluctuate, and how people treat us, we expect good things from God because he has promised good things. We believe by faith that he is leading us where he wants us to go. We thank him for his provision because we trust that he has given it graciously. And we don't let worry or fear enter our minds because we know we're safely in his hand.

The opposite of trust in everyday life is pessimistic thinking, negative talk, and low-grade suspicion that things will inevitably go wrong. When we're constantly a little on edge, agitated with those around us, bored with life, and discouraged about our prospects, we aren't trusting God. That may seem like a harsh assessment, but it's true. Trust, in the normal course of life, is a general attitude that expects goodness from God's hand.

This is the basic level of trust, and it should come fairly naturally to us when we're regularly in God's Word and able to worship him for who he is. We'll have to contend for this kind of trust to a degree, but not as much as we will when we're in a crisis.

Crisis trust. Traumatic situations require a deeper trust because in such times circumstances use a megaphone to report the disaster that's coming into our lives. In a crisis, we have plenty of voices telling us negative news and few telling us that God is trustworthy. This is when we need to remind ourselves repeatedly of the things he has told us—that all things work together for the good of those who love him,[32] that he has plans for us for good and not for disaster,[33] and all of those well-known verses we rely on so heavily. Sometimes repeating these verses to ourselves sounds like we're trying to convince ourselves of something that isn't true, but that isn't the case. We're actually convincing ourselves of what *is* true, and it takes some serious convincing because we've listened to quite a few lies during the course of our lives. These are the times when God stretches our capacity to believe him. It may hurt, but it builds our faith.

The opposite of this kind of trust is anxiety and panic. When a crisis or predicament hits us, our natural tendency is to think of all the possible negative implications. We feel threatened. We worry about all the variables involved. We wonder what's going to happen to us. In reality, God frequently uses crises to pro- voke better situations in the lives of his people than they were experiencing before— biblical crises almost always turned out elevating those who went through them in faith.[34] But our first thoughts aren't what good God is about to accomplish through crisis; they're what hardships might come from it. We have to learn how to trust God to use crises as catalytic events in our lives.

> **We have to learn how to trust God to use crises as catalytic events in our lives.**

Desperate trust. A third kind of trust takes crisis a step further. It comes not when our welfares seem up in the air but in the aftermath of our worst-case scenarios. The issue is whether we can trust God in spite of our griefs and in the midst of what seems like disaster. We reassure ourselves with the same verses we used when the crisis was still pending, but God's goodness is harder to see when everything else looks dark. When it seems like his will is clearly not being done, can we trust that somehow it still is? That's a fierce battle that we usually have to fight when we have the least energy to fight it. Trust in the midst of grief usually looks like we're barely hanging on. But God is just as pleased with that as he would be if we were bravely charging against Goliath with full confidence that he would give us victory.

The opposite of trust in dark times is despair. Grief is normal and even godly, but despair is never God's will for us. Our natural reaction is to wonder if God has forgotten us or perhaps even judged us harshly. His desire, however, is for us to look to him in trust even in the worst of times. He doesn't promise to spare us from trouble; he promises to be our refuge until the storms pass.[35] Faith is never stretched and tested like it is in a calamity. But God will respond faithfully to those who trust him anyway.

Specific trust. Another kind of trust involves believing God for something he has specifically promised us. When we've prayed a request and received a confirmation from him by faith—relevant and pointed Bible verses brought to our attention, a timely word in sermons or from other believers, outward signs that confirm God's voice to us, the repeated whisper of his Spirit in our hearts, and any of the other ways he speaks—we frequently experience a waiting period in which trust is tested and strengthened and ripped apart and rebuilt and strengthened some more. During this gap between promise and fulfillment, we question whether we understood the promise correctly, whether we asked according to God's will, whether he will really follow through with what we thought he said, and a host of other variables that seem to undermine our faith—or, if we will let them, strengthen it. The wait itself can become a battleground, as can every word or event related to our situation during this time. Regardless of how things turn out, or how we expect them to turn out, God wants us to rest in him throughout the process by maintaining our trust that he is good and is working on our behalf.

How Trust Grows

There's nothing wrong with having degrees of trust for varying situations, and there's nothing sinful about having your trust tested. In fact, it will be. It's the only way for trust to grow. But we can do some things practically to cultivate trust. Even in times when we have little or no trust to begin with, we can move to a position of great trust and rest in God. It takes an intentional effort and a resolve not to give up easily, but we can increase our trust with several effective practices:

Confess. We don't like to think of our anxieties and fears as sinful attitudes, but they do fly in the face of several direct instructions and fall far short of God's intention for us. They are understandable flaws, but they still need to be confessed. When we acknowledge that our worries come from a heart of unbelief, God is more than willing to forgive, cleanse, and heal.

In order to confess our mistrust, sometimes we need to dig deep to find the root of it. The best way to do that is to keep asking questions and follow where they lead: *What am I really worried about in this situation? Why do I think God might let me down? What would happen if things don't turn out as I want them to? Am I worried that God might abandon me in my disappointment? Am I afraid that he won't give me grace for hard or unexpected situations? What if the very worst happens—will he meet me there?*

We often find after answering a series of questions like this that our mistrust isn't so much about God letting us go through hard things but about having to go through them without his strength or reassurances or provision. We envision a crisis that isn't accompanied by his presence. But scripturally this is an impossibility for those who trust him. We have to confess our suspicions that God might forsake us in a time of need.

Ask. It's amazing how rarely it occurs to us to ask for attributes like faith and trust. We're used to asking for other things and then trying to work up the faith to pray for them and the trust to expect them. But the flesh can trust God only very imperfectly; the Spirit within us can accomplish spiritual attitudes far better than we ever can. We're supposed to come to him for all of our needs, and we definitely need to trust him. The next step in growing trust is to ask God for it.

There are two sides to this. One is asking him to remove our unbelief, mistrust, fears, anxieties, worries, and negative expectations. The other is to ask him to empower us to believe, trust, be courageous, be at peace, and expect great things from him. He'll address both ends of the spectrum— the junk that needs to go and the attitudes we need to develop. His Spirit will stir up the right perspectives within us when we ask him to.

Acknowledge. The Bible doesn't just tell us to trust God. It tells us to trust him *because . . .* It gives us plenty of reasons to believe he's trustworthy. When we acknowledge who God is and remind ourselves of his love, his wisdom, his power, his faithfulness, and everything else he represents, our level of trust soars. When we're in conflict, we need to confess him as our Defender and our Peace. When we're sick, we need to confess him as our Healer. When we desire to be rescued, we need to confess him as our Deliverer. If our underlying problem is mistrust, acknowledging the greatness of the one we're dealing with is a necessary part of the solution. The fallacy of mistrust is that it doesn't recognize God for who he is. We need to bring our false perceptions to the surface and contradict them with truth.

Think. I was recently going through an epic battle to trust God on a particular issue, and I felt like I was losing. The "yes, but" tendency can be strong in me. I'm not sure why, but I approach certain promises from God as though he's a bait-and-switch deity with plenty of legal loopholes that would allow him at any given moment, no matter how much I trust him to answer a specific prayer, to tell me, "Oh, I'm sorry, Chris. You misunderstood. That's not what my promise means. That isn't what I intended for you. I know you sought my will zealously and listened intently, and I know you took some clear Scripture verses and timely signs as indications of my will, hanging on my every word and absorbing every encouragement you could find, but you missed the fine print. I'm too mysterious for you to relate to. You tried to understand what I was saying, but you just didn't get it. My yes doesn't actually mean yes, and my no doesn't really mean no. True, I'm a rewarder of those who seek me, but I don't define *reward* the way you do. It's okay—you'll understand when you get to heaven." I know those are slanderous thoughts, and putting them down on paper embarrasses me—would God really treat his children so carelessly and even deceptively?—but if you've had battles with trust, you know the gymnastics your mind

> If you've had battles with trust, you know the gymnastics your mind can go through to question God's faithfulness.

can go through to question God's faithfulness. And in this particular season regarding this particular issue, my mind was extremely active.

By God's provision and design, I was scheduled to write two study guides during this time, one on the life of Abraham and one on the topic of faith. And, as I sometimes do, I booked a hotel room in order to write practically nonstop for a week. I checked into the hotel under extreme mental stress about God's promises and how they related to my prayer requests, and left a week later as calm and assured as I've ever been about a matter of faith. Why? Because focusing on God's faithfulness as revealed in his Word has a powerful effect on our minds.

A week of studying Abraham and faith altered my perspective and built trust. Nothing changed in my circumstances during that week, but my heart found a place of rest as God spoke through his Word every day. I grew more confident in him. And though most people don't have the opportunity to spend a week in isolation examining a single section of Scripture, we all have access to the same truths. Digging into them and letting God speak through them can literally change the way we think. It can undo the lies that cause us to question God and magnify the truths that enable us to trust him.

Speak. This sounds like a psychological technique, but it's really a powerful spiritual tool. Incorporating words of trust into our conversations—including the conversations we have with ourselves—has a dramatic impact on the way we think and on what ultimately sinks into our hearts. That's because our brains respond to one voice above all others: our own. That's the way we're wired. When we tell ourselves things never work out the way we want them to, our brains believe us. But when we tell ourselves that God is working on a good plan and will come through for us, we believe that instead. It takes time—we have a long history of negative self-talk to overcome—but it works.

Remember, you aren't trying to convince yourself of something that isn't true. You're trying to undo the lies you've believed and convince yourself of something that *is* true. There is spiritual influence in the spoken word; a superficial reading of Genesis 1:3 and similar verses should convince you of that. That's why Proverbs says the tongue has the power of life and death[36] and why Jesus told his disciples to speak to mountains.[37] Spoken words accomplish a lot, even when you're the only one listening. Don't catch yourself talking about how dire your situation is, as though God weren't involved in it. Affirm your trust again and again and again.

Testimonies of Trust

We can see these practices in various places in our "field manual," the Psalms. We can also see many of them at work in biblical characters who demonstrate the levels of trust we identified above:

Everyday trust. Paul seemed to expect God to do good things, even when he didn't know exactly what those good things would be. He asked God for boldness, wrote words expressing great confidence in God's purposes, and often acknowledged the glory and majesty of the God he served. In trust, he expected to be guided to the places he needed to go;[38] he expected God to continue to work in the people who had come to faith;[39] he was confident that God would use the preaching of others, even when that preaching came out of wrong motives;[40] and he trusted that Jesus would be exalted in his body whether he lived or died.[41] We see practically no hints that Paul was worried about God's ability to handle his situations, even though he was in quite a few predicaments during the course of his ministry. In fact, he did radically trusting things like sing praises in prison and go to Jerusalem even when warned that serious trouble awaited him there. We might call that reckless, but God called it faith. And he blessed Paul's ministry in remarkable ways.

Crisis trust. An enemy of the Jews managed to convince the king of Persia to pass a royal decree to wipe them out. The situation looked hopeless, but God had positioned Esther years earlier to be in the right place at the right time. Her cousin Mordecai had to give her some prompts to get her into an attitude of willingness because Esther didn't immediately have confidence that God was doing something good. But she called a fast, faithfully moved forward, and watched God not only save his people from a major crisis but use that crisis to enhance his people's position in the empire. In fact, the very enemies that caused such anxiety and fear in the hearts of Jews were eliminated by the way God reversed their plans. What looked at first like a cause of great grief turned into Judaism's most wildly celebrated holiday on the annual calendar. That's what trust during a crisis can accomplish.

Desperate trust. Job had every reason to ditch his faith in God. In fact, that's exactly what his wife urged him to do.[42] After all, God had allowed all his property to be destroyed, all his children to be killed, and his health to waste away. Even so, Job spoke words that affirmed his trust in God: "I know that my Redeemer lives, and that in the end he will stand upon the earth. And after my skin has been destroyed, yet in my flesh I will see God; I myself will see him with my own eyes—I, and not another. How my heart yearns within me!"[43] Though he didn't understand what was happening to him and even confessed mistrust at times, by the end of the book God honored his faithfulness and rearranged his perspective. The book begins and ends with Job as a blessed and faithful worshiper.

Specific trust. Abraham waited twenty-five years between the promise God gave him and the fulfillment that ultimately came. During that time, he remained faithful and waited for the promise. The testimony of New Testament writers was that he did not waver in unbelief[44] but instead looked forward to the city with foundations designed by God.[45] We know from Genesis that Abraham questioned and stumbled a few times, but he continued to look to God, and God continued to encourage him and confirm his covenant. Abraham came to see God as his "shield" and his "exceedingly great reward,"[46] and as his provider.[47] The covenant specified that all the nations of the world would be blessed by Abraham's descendants.[48] And because he trusted, they have been.

All of these heroes of faith had ample opportunity to mistrust God. They went through excruciatingly long waits, severe crises, and extreme hardships. I wonder sometimes how history and Scripture would remember them if they had allowed worry and fear to consume them. They certainly understood those attitudes; they were entirely human. But they didn't hold on to their fears. At some point, they each made a decision to trust God in spite of the threats coming against them, in spite of the circumstances they had to endure, and in spite of the fears and worries of those around them. They saw beyond their situations and held on to God.

We make the mistake sometimes of thinking these people were more naturally predisposed to trust than we are. But it didn't come easier for them than it does for us. They chose the attitude they would have toward God. They embraced his promises and his plans in spite of plenty of reasons not to. They made a decision about where to invest their trust. And, as a result, they overcame the burdens that tried to weigh them down.

Please don't misunderstand. God allows his people to

experience the burdens of life. These biblical heroes didn't live completely weightlessly. We can't say they didn't have a care in the world. They certainly did. They faced enormous crises. But those same crises would have crushed people who had little or no faith, or who chose not to take their burdens to God. These scriptural characters brought their adversity to God, trusted him with it, and came out profoundly strengthened and able to handle life with a peace most people never know.

That can be your testimony too. As trust increases in your life, God will respond to it with more opportunities for service, a greater sense of his presence, and the kind of blessings he gives only to those who have faith. Trust will positively affect your mood, your relationships, and your health. It will make you feel lighter even when people around you are stumbling under lesser weights than the ones you bear. Ultimately, it will enable you to live with a sense of strength and freedom.

CHAPTER 5

RELEASE

I LOVE BEACHES. I always have, and I always will. I think they're pretty close to paradise, and I'm convinced heaven will be full of them.

My family usually takes a summer trip to the beach, but we couldn't squeeze it in last summer. The schedule was too hectic, the workload was too urgent, and the time went by faster than ever, so we missed our trip. I think I missed it the most.

I'm not quite sure why I love the beach so much, but I think it has something to do with the total convergence of sights and smells and sounds that, if I experienced them separately, would be only mildly pleasant. My favorite color is that soothing aqua that almost begs you to go snorkeling; my favorite temperature is eighty-seven degrees, give or take about ten; my favorite smell is coconut; my favorite sound is the rhythmic pulse of wave meeting shore; my favorite exercise is rowing a kayak against the surf; my favorite footwear is none; and two of my favorite feelings are cool water and a warm breeze. Put them all together, and I'm in sensory heaven.

Throughout the year, I see aqua in a few photographs, I smell coconut when I wash what's left of my hair, I feel an occasional warm breeze, and I relish eighty-seven-degree days several times between May and September. Every time, I enjoy the sensation and I'm reminded of paradise. But there's nothing like bringing all of those pleasures into one moment. All of my senses celebrate in unison at the beach. That's why I love it so much; it's a total experience.

Since I can't live at the beach at this point in my life, I have ways of bringing the beach to me. The screen savers on my computer are all pictures of French Polynesia. The background image on my cell phone is a sliver of sand and palm trees surrounded by calm, Caribbean blue. My phone's ringtone is a catchy little reggae tune.

Over time, my love of beaches has grown into a vision. It's me living on beachfront property, relaxing in a stress-free environment, and enjoying nature the way God intended for it to be enjoyed. I don't have an irresponsible, "don't worry, be happy" attitude in this vision, and I'm not lazy in it either. Not at all. In fact, I'm as productive as I've ever been. I write every morning for several hours and experience life every afternoon and evening so I can write some more about life the next day. It's a simple but efficient rhythm. I'm convinced it could work.

As you probably noticed, there are no burdens in this vision. Responsibilities, to be sure, but no heavy weights dragging me down. I certainly see myself sharing life with people I love, and I know that involves plenty of attachments and concerns. But somehow there's a freedom in this picture that isn't lessened by messy circumstances. The way I see it, it's possible to go through life without being dragged down by it.

I realize that my vision has some unrealistic thinking behind it. For example, if that kind of life is really attainable, why am I not living it now? Would the locale make that much of a difference? Obviously not—some other factors would have to be involved, not the least of which would be a higher level of income to make it possible. But I'm not quite willing to force my vision to bow to my current experience and definition of "reality." I believe there are some ways, at least in part, to make current experience and reality comply with this vision. One of those ways is to simply let go of my heavy cargo.

Unloading

When Christian is first introduced in *The Pilgrim's Progress,* he is clothed in rags, holding a book in his hand, and bearing a great burden on his back. Because of the distress of this burden, he cannot even enjoy his home and family. He meets a man named Evangelist, who tells him of a place he can go to have life and be relieved of his burden. And thus begins his famous allegorical journey in the ways of the Kingdom of God.

At one point early in his journey, after Christian laments the slow progress he is making because of his burden, he and his companion, Pliable, fall into a bog called Despond. Weighed down by his load, Christian sinks deep into the mire and is abandoned by his fickle friend to struggle out on his own. Along the way, he is offered shortcuts and alternatives that promise to relieve him of his burden, but none have any effect. Mr. Worldly Wiseman assures him that his troubles are only beginning if he continues on his journey, but Christian is convinced that his burden is more terrible than any pain, hunger, danger, dragon, darkness, or death he could encounter. His only option is to continue toward the gate that Evangelist told him about.

Finally, Christian comes to a path walled on each side by Salvation, and at the top of that path stands a cross next to a grave. As soon as he encounters the cross, his burden falls from his shoulders, rolls down his back, and tumbles into the grave. Christian's heart suddenly feels light and happy. His burden is gone forever.

It's clear that John Bunyan meant for Christian's burden to illustrate our weight of sin and guilt and for the cross to represent the forgiveness that looses the burden from our backs. And that kind of burden is truly the core issue of the gospel. But Jesus came to deal not only with our sin but also with the effects of our sin, including the undue stresses and strains our other burdens cause. In fact, all we receive in the Kingdom of God comes to us through the Cross. Bunyan's picture is a great illustration of what happens when we come to the Cross for any reason. And Christian's release of his burden is an inspiring picture of our desires to unload our baggage of any kind.

Most people who feel weighed down by life would love to have an experience like Christian's—a moment in time when they could dump everything into a bottomless abyss and never have to deal with it again. And we know from prophecies and promises that a day for that is coming. But we also know that while we continue to live in a fallen world, life doesn't exactly work that way, no matter how thoroughly we've been redeemed. We can't shed all of our responsibilities and obligations. We have decisions to make, tasks to perform, things to learn, bills to pay, and people to care for. We don't live in a vacuum.

> **Jesus came to deal not only with our sin but also with the effects of our sin, including the undue stresses and strains our other burdens cause.**

We can, however, cast all our cares on the Lord. That's a promise—or, rather, a command.[1] It's an act of rolling our worries off our shoulders and onto his, fully expecting him to take responsibility for dealing with them appropriately. We absolve ourselves of the responsibility for determining an outcome and handle only the aspects of those burdens that he tells us to handle. In other words, we give up ownership of our issues to him, and then we steward them however he directs us to. We become property managers for the problems we used to own.

Why don't more people do this? One reason is that issue of trust we talked about in the last chapter—it requires a huge amount of faith to actually let go of our junk—but another is the fact that it never occurs to us that we can. Few people realize what God offers us when we give ourselves to him. We aren't just trusting him for salvation from sin and shame and guilt; we're trusting him with the complete ownership of our lives. When we surrender ourselves to his will, we surrender *everything*. Even our worst junk and our hardest, most draining problems.

What would happen, then, if we just let go? What if we refused to worry, be anxious, fear the future, obsess about difficulties, panic, brood, get flustered, be annoyed, get agitated, or wonder "what if" about every negative possibility? What would happen if we acknowledged every real problem and care but then asked God to deal with each one and really believed he would? How would life look if we simply decided that we would live with a sense of freedom and abandon?

The picture that comes to mind when I think about letting go is of me hanging on to the edge of a building, with my only chance of survival being the safety net spread out ten stories below. I know in my head I should let go, but the whole falling business terrifies me. Hanging on is strenuous and will eventually wear me out. And the net below *seems* to be strong and secure enough to hold my weight and keep me from hitting the pavement. But to actually choose to hurtle helplessly a hundred feet through the air goes against my nature.

That's essentially the choice we face with our burdens. It seems illogical and unnatural to let them go, but doing so is really our only chance of living the life we were intended to live. We hang on because we're terrified. What if our deepest desires and basic needs fall to the ground? What if we only *thought* we saw a net down below us? What if God doesn't catch us? The result would be disastrous. We would crash painfully and permanently.

The truth is that God promises the safety net of his love and care. Our question above—what would happen if we just let go—has a sure and certain answer. We don't need to worry or be afraid. We *can* live in freedom from the things that weigh us down. We simply need to decide to let go.

An Unusual Death

I believe that a sense of freedom and abandon is an integral part of the gospel. We generally read statements like "take up your cross"[2] and "I have been crucified with Christ"[3] as commands to sacrifice ourselves and our agendas for the sake of the Kingdom. In other words, we see them as chores and disciplines, but they are also an invitation, a golden opportunity to stop living out of our own strength. They offer us a chance to walk away from our cares.

Do you realize what this opportunity means? The reason our burdens weigh us down and drain us of strength is that we depend on either our own resources or the cruelty of chance and fate to deal with them. The Cross of Jesus, which looks like death to us, is essentially a release from that futile condition. Though many Christians perceive the Cross as a death of our entire personalities, all desires, and any sense of individuality—in other words, we basically become empty shells for the Spirit to inhabit—that isn't the biblical message at all. God made us in his image and keeps us intact when he saves us. The death we experience is really death to a way of life. We no longer rely on our own strength. We no longer depend on our own ingenuity, skills, assets, or energy. We have another fountain of strength to draw from, a higher wisdom to follow. We essentially sign over the title deed to a new owner and use his resources for our fuel and support.

This is what many have referred to as the exchanged life. The biographers of Hudson Taylor, that great pioneer missionary to China's interior, called the exchanged life his "spiritual secret." After about fifteen years of ministry more fruitful than most of us could hope to have in a lifetime, Taylor realized that he had been striving in his own strength—i.e., carrying his own burdens—rather than simply being a branch on the Vine. This truth of how branches abide on the vine and how one can be crucified with Christ came to him, via a friend in a similar position, when he was burned-out and at the end of his rope. He had spent himself to spread the gospel in China, and he was tired and frustrated with how drained he had become in serving Jesus. There had to be a better way.

Taylor's spiritual secret of simply resting in Jesus was as transforming a revelation to him as the moment he first accepted Christ. He finally "saw" what he had been looking for—the life of Jesus living and working through him. Galatians 2:20 became a reality; he fully identified with his crucifixion with Jesus and could say with confidence that he, Taylor, no longer lived, but Christ lived in him. He still had his personality, his mission, and his awareness of the people and things around him, but the life that was in him came from another source.

The seventeenth-century French theologian François Fénelon wrote often of our crucifixion with Jesus and saw our "death" as the key to life—though he focused much more on the death side of the equation than on the resurrected life of Jesus within us. He emphasized that dead people don't get offended, strive for their own fulfillment, get caught up in petty squabbles, and so on. In both his and Taylor's minds, the way to freedom is simply to let go of all that weighs us down.

Ironically, pursuing this exchanged life of a crucified self who is empowered by a risen Lord can become its own sort of striving if we aren't careful. We can try to achieve it in the strength of the flesh, which defeats the whole purpose. On the other hand, it's also possible in letting go of our loads to assume that we no longer play a part in the lives we live. I've read critics of the exchanged-life approach who assert that a passive lifestyle is completely unbiblical. They have tried it, they say, and found that just sitting there waiting for Jesus to live his life in you doesn't work. But any cursory look at Taylor's life would prove that he was never talking about passivity. He was as active after this revelation of the exchanged life as he was before. The difference is in the source of our energy for living. If we try to carry our burdens and accomplish our goals in the strength of our flesh, we'll fail and burn out. If we transfer our loads onto Jesus himself, we'll find that he is actually there to carry them. This is more than a mental trick; there's a real Spirit willing to work on our behalf. But we have to see ourselves—really *perceive* ourselves—as people who have given up our own strength and who function completely out of his. That picture of relying on another has to fully sink in until we live with that attitude and awareness.

Taylor's description of the result whets an insatiable appetite in me for this way of life:

The sweetest part, if one may speak of one part
being sweeter than another, is the rest which full
identification with Christ brings. I am no longer
anxious about anything, as I realize this; for He,
I know, is able to carry out His will, and His will is
mine. It makes no matter where He places me, or
how. That is rather for Him to consider than for me;

for in the easiest position He must give me His grace, and in the most difficult His grace is sufficient. . . . So, if God should place me in serious perplexity, must He not give me much guidance; in positions of great difficulty, much grace; in circumstances of great pressure and trials, much strength? No fear that His resources will prove unequal to the emergency! And His resources are mine, for He is mine, and is with me and dwells in me.[4]

This is the *shalom* we seek, the peace we lost in Eden. We long for this kind of rest. And we can have it, even if we carry responsibility for the lives of a hundred people. Taylor had already founded the China Inland Mission when he discovered what it meant to be crucified with Jesus, and he oversaw a number of missionary families and made monumental decisions regarding the agency's work. As part of a "faith" mission, none of his workers ever had a padded bank account or knew whether their next donation would come on time or even come at all. Still, Taylor found peace in the midst of the difficulty of mission work, anti-Western hostility and persecution, and financial challenges. The level of responsibility didn't matter; the level of surrender did. He found that he could let go of all of his striving because Jesus would actually live a supernatural life within him.

Think of how it would play out in our lives if we really believed this. For one thing, we wouldn't feel the need to arrange our own affairs and work out our own futures. This "need" is behind a lot of our cares and concerns. We may trust God to work out our lives the way *he* wants to, but if we have a sneaking suspicion that his will won't look anything like we want it to, we'll find ourselves strategizing about how to get our own desires fulfilled. The Cross eliminates the need to do that. We can only surrender our wills to his to the degree that we trust him; and for our loads to feel any lighter, that has to amount to quite a bit. But that's the goal: deep-down trust that can count on his agenda to be at least as good as or better than our own. Then we can relinquish ours and rest in his.

When we no longer have to rely on ourselves to push an agenda, we also find that we no longer have to defend our own rights. This takes a lot of trust, too, but we can depend on God to put us where he wants us and to protect us from the offenses and injustices he wants to protect us from. If we belong to him, he will defend us as needed. If we find that he isn't—that he is letting us experience some injustices—then we can know that he has a purpose for them.

We see this principle in Scripture quite often. Joseph was betrayed by his brothers in one of the worst injustices in Hebrew Scripture, but God ordained that betrayal in order to save a nation. Paul and Silas were unjustly thrown in prison, but God used that event as a catalyst to help establish one of the New Testament's strongest churches and to impact Philippi with the gospel. And, most conspicuously, God sent Jesus into the world for the specific purpose of experiencing history's most heinous injustice as the key to redeeming his fallen creation. When we don't lay down our own defenses, such miracles don't happen nearly as often. But when we do, God can change the world through us.

This is only the beginning. When we decide to let go, we no longer need to work on our reputations, maintain our expectations, hedge our bets in case God doesn't answer our prayers, strive to get all our needs met, and worry about all the ways our agendas might not happen if we aren't zealous to stay on top of them. Being a branch that is fed by the Vine is a liberating role to play in every area of life.

That's why this surrender, which feels very much like death at first, is really the beginning of life. It can be frightening to surrender everything our hearts treasure to the hands of a God who, as we've been told perhaps too often, is focused on his purposes and not ours. What we don't realize is that, as he works his purpose in us, the treasures of our hearts are often actually those he has placed there and fully intends to satisfy. The ones that aren't there by his design are either stripped of their power or are met with more than enough grace for us to bear their loss. We may die the death of surrender, but we're quickly filled with much of what we wanted and more. Our fears are, in a sense, well-founded; surrender is, after all, a real surrender. But in another sense, our fears are lying to us. The benefits of surrender are well worth the cost.

Humility

We can't make the decision to let go of the ownership (and therefore the burdens) of our lives while maintaining any sense of pride in ourselves. Pride is a form of self-life, and the self-life is never willing to die. When we have a strong sense of personal agenda, reputation, status, and so on, we have a lot to lose if God takes us up on our offers of giving it all to him. This is one reason God opposes the proud so strenuously in Scripture; they put themselves in a position of being unusable to him and ultimately unsatisfying to themselves. He can't fulfill his good purposes in someone who is filled with lesser purposes.

Pride is a heavy burden—actually a heavy package of many burdens—but its opposite, humility, is easy to bear.

> When we have a strong sense of personal agenda, reputation, and status, we have a lot to lose if God takes us up on our offers of giving it all to him.

Humility may offend the ego, but it isn't a complicated or exhausting way of life. How much energy do you need to spend to defend a low position or unassuming attitude? Virtually none. It's a very free way to live.

A story told of William Carey illustrates the ease of humility. This "father of modern missions" would become a historically great figure, but when he first arrived in India, he was looked upon with contempt by many British dignitaries who already lived there. Once at a dinner party, a guest seemingly attempted to embarrass the young missionary by asking loudly whether it was true that he once worked as a lowly shoemaker. Carey answered without any offense. "No, your lordship, not a shoemaker, only a cobbler"—the even lower position of mending rather than making shoes.

Carey could have said something like, "Actually, I spent several years as a leader in the footwear design industry," or some other such padded statement that cast him in a better light. I've done similar things in the past, pretending to know things I didn't know rather than owning up to the fact that I might not be as educated or intelligent as I wanted to appear. I don't know why I would think it's better to fabricate an answer that might be right rather than simply admit I don't know, but I used to do that quite a bit, and I know I'm not alone. Most of us find ourselves posing in certain situations to appear better or wealthier or more intelligent or more well-connected than we are. We bring the spirit and language of a résumé into our daily conversations.

Why do we care what people think of us? Do we need them to tell us we're "somebody" because we aren't sure we really are? Is God's stamp of approval on his own creation and the image he put within us really that insignificant to us? I don't know what the roots of our ego needs are—I'm sure they differ from person to person—but our posturing and image crafting are really unnecessary. It seems we would have noticed at some point that the most respected people are not those with the best image but those who come across as completely authentic. That's who others look up to.

It requires a lot of energy to come up with a creative spin on oneself and then maintain it in a variety of situations thereafter. (Just ask anyone who got a job with an inflated résumé and then had to live up to the inflated expectations that came along with it.) Managing your own PR can be a full-time job.

Owning up to who you are, where you've been, and what you've done without any pretense . . . well, that's a piece of cake. It's simply a choice between stroking the ego and living free.

> **The most respected people are not those with the best image but those who come across as completely authentic.**

Humility is a light burden. There's no image to protect, no status to maintain, nothing to prove. It's a valued virtue in the Kingdom of God and, in fact, a characteristic of God himself. We normally don't see God as humble because he wants to be praised and is zealous for the glory of his name. But God's desire for his own glory isn't pride, it's realism. He's the highest value and the greatest being in all of existence. Even our best worship is an understatement of who he is. Still, he is portrayed as humble. His Son, the exact representation of the Father,[5] is described as a meek and gentle Servant in prophecies of Isaiah and in descriptions of his ministry in the gospels.

The humility of Jesus is the theme of one of the best-known passages of the New Testament: the Christ hymn of Philippians 2:6-11. As that chapter begins, Paul is urging the church to "be humble, thinking of others as better than yourselves,"[6] and the primary example of this attitude is Jesus. It's hard to imagine the Son of God thinking of others as better than himself, but this is the attitude Paul says Jesus had.

Though he was God, he did not demand and cling to his rights as God. He made himself nothing; he took the humble position of a slave and appeared in human form. And in human form he obediently humbled himself even further by dying a criminal's death on a cross. Because of this, God raised him up to the heights of heaven and gave him a name that is above every other name, so that at the name of Jesus every knee will bow, in heaven and on earth and under the earth, and every tongue will confess that Jesus Christ is Lord, to the glory of God the Father.

Jesus perfectly modeled what it looks like for a human being to live in humility. He refused to defend himself and never worked to maintain his reputation. He did not pose, spin his words, or cultivate an image. The result? God defended him—raised him up to the heights of heaven—and established his glory forever.

If ever we needed proof that we don't need to worry about our own status or welfare, this is it. One might counter that God allowed Jesus to be executed, but when we trust God, we don't rebel even against negative circumstances that he ordains. We know that his ultimate purposes are good. Even when events seem threatening, we can look past them toward the blessings God has promised. But we can't pick up our own agendas again. In humility, we make a declaration of dependence and stick with it.

I had an opportunity to practice some blunt honesty about myself at work the morning before I started writing this chapter. One of my bosses approached me about assuming an expanded role with a project we've been working on. A team member is leaving our ministry for another position, and someone needs to step in to be the point person for communicating with one of our clients. In former days, I might have seized the opportunity for greater responsibility; it would make me look good to the higher-ups, increase my job security, boost a future résumé, and so on. But I've decided over the last few years that I don't need to position myself. I can trust God to do that. So I told my boss that I have some serious weaknesses in the area in which he wanted to increase my responsibility. I'm good at writing but not at communicating with clients. In fact, I tend to let a lot of phone calls and e-mails slip through the cracks. I'm working on it—I realize it's a huge character flaw. And if the ministry really needed me to step into that role, I would gladly do it to the best of my ability. But he deserved to know that my ability is lacking.

I think my boss respected the honest assessment. He said he didn't want me working outside my areas of giftedness, and though I might need to do some things to fill in for the departing employee, he would look for someone else to perform those tasks in the long run. The conversation ended with both of us feeling respected and better equipped to proceed in the right direction.

There are times when we have to step into roles that will stretch us, and I was perfectly willing to do that in this situation. But what if I had portrayed myself as capable in an area in which I'm not? And what if my boss gave me a new role with the expectation that I was exactly the right person for it? Sure, I would be able to put it on a résumé one day, but I would also spend the next few months or years scrambling to maintain a pose, doing less-than-excellent work, and frustrating myself and the people around me. It was much easier to say, "I'm good at these things and terrible at these other things, so fit me into the ministry's needs however you want." And if he decided to put me in that role anyway, I could handle it with no pressure to be someone I'm not because I had already been completely honest about my skills. There's no pressure in that approach, no unnecessary burden to carry, and everyone wins.

It should be clear that this attitude isn't necessarily easy to maintain in every situation. It takes practice. But it should also be clear that it isn't heavy. It's much less burdensome than the alternative—a lifestyle of pride and the endless exertion that requires. A humble heart is free to relax and trust God with whatever happens, knowing that whatever happens is under his watch.

Shedding Layers

Eustace Clarence Scrubb, a character in C. S. Lewis's *The Voyage of the Dawn Treader*, was a proud, pretentious boy when he was first pulled against his will into Narnia. He complained constantly, insisted on pushing his agenda on everyone else, and expected others to comply with his demands. But Eustace changed dramatically through one frightening experience. Shipwrecked with his friends on an island, he turned into a dragon—a true reflection of the way he had been behaving.

As a dragon, Eustace began to realize how perfectly beastly he had been acting. He felt isolated from his friends, even though they tried to accept him as a dragon, and could only wish he had treated everyone more nicely when he had the chance. One night, Eustace was awakened by the lion Aslan, who led him to a well on a mountaintop and prompted him to begin shedding his reptilian skin and scales. Several superficial molts didn't transform Eustace's nature, but a deep cutting away of his skin by Aslan and a bath in the well restored his original form. Eustace was again a boy, but now a nicer, gentler one. He became compliant, unpretentious, and generous for the rest of the journey.

Our transformation from burdened to unburdened people may not involve the change of character necessary to Eustace's transformation, but it certainly involves shedding a lot of excess baggage and dropping some external appearances. It may seem obvious to say this, but when we let go, we actually have to let go. The intention to let go isn't enough. A few attempts at letting go are not enough. A wish or prayer to let go isn't enough. We have to lay some things down. And sometimes that feels like peeling off part of who we are, not

> **It may seem obvious, but when we let go, we actually have to let go. The intention to let go isn't enough.**

once but repeatedly. It can be as uncomfortable as a dragon shedding its skin.

What exactly do we lay down when we let go of the self-life? Like Eustace, we may have to let go of some expectations, some demands, and some attitudes.

We've discussed the burden of expectations quite a bit, but I should make it clear that we aren't talking about laying down *all* expectations. A life without expectations would be a life without faith or hope. We don't want that. What we do want is a life without agendas that aren't going to get fulfilled or that don't match God's purposes. We want to get rid of wrong, misplaced, distorted, and self-centered expectations. Those are the ones that weigh us down the most.

The flip side of letting go of our expectations is letting go of the expectations other people have placed on us. We often feel obligated to fulfill others' desires and needs simply because they expect us to. While we don't want to neglect our real responsibilities, we also can't live by the dictates of the people around us. Just because someone expects us to do something doesn't mean we have to. We are obligated to serve God and serve others the way he leads us to—not the way they tell us to.

We have to get pretty defiant about sticking only with God's expectations of us and not giving in to others' demands. It takes a strong sense of devotion to him and an insistence that he's the primary focus of our lives. When we don't understand how he values and affirms us and are used to depending instead on the affirmation of others, it's virtually impossible to live free from misplaced demands. We become conflict avoiders and people pleasers. That's a hectic, heavy way of life that never catches up to all the obligations we think we have. We never feel settled until we know that we ultimately serve God alone.

One indicator of the expectations others have placed on us is how easily and in which areas they feel offended when we fail to meet them. I've known people who assume that if I don't answer my cell phone, I'm screening my calls and have chosen not to respond to them. The possibility that I might be in a meeting or am recharging my phone or am extremely busy with an urgent situation doesn't seem to occur to them. That's a misplaced offense. I've also received gifts that, as it turns out, weren't really gifts at all but an expectation that I would be indebted to the giver for some future, unspecified service or allegiance. When I unwittingly fail to deliver on my "debt," the history of the relationship is recited to prove how ungrateful or irresponsible I am. Fortunately, most of the world doesn't function this way, but you and I both know people who do. When a perceived slight occurs and there are a hundred different possible explanations for it, some people tend to gravitate toward the most offensive possibility and then steam about it.

As an editor of several publications over the years, I've received numerous letters and e-mails from people who felt slighted by the way something was worded, by my or another writer's opinions, by how girlish or manly or childish or archaic or overly trendy the graphic design was, and by how late their publications arrived. Sometimes these complaints were quite legitimate, stemming from reasonable expectations. Others were part of a normal conversation about ideas and events in a public forum. But sometimes there were clearly some personal issues beneath the surface. Either way, in every case, the degree to which the reader was offended was a clear reflection of how strong his or her expectations were.

I like getting letters; it shows that people are reading and engaging with ideas. But some people engage in a way that reveals their wounds. For example, when I get a five-page handwritten letter about a passing comment in an article that was taken the wrong way, I know I've triggered some distress or misdirected need in the letter writer. When someone responds to a simple mistake with a vitriolic e-mail filled with accusations of sloppiness or error, there's something wrong underneath the surface, especially when that mistake in no way affects the quality of that person's life or anyone else's. Try reading the letters to the editor in a local newspaper with this in mind. You can usually tell when people are reacting out of their own issues and when they are disagreeing in a healthy way. When they are reacting out of their personal issues, they are invariably carrying burdens they were never designed to carry. Only people who feel free are able to live with a sense of grace toward others. A disproportionate attitude of negativity, bitterness, or indignation is almost always an indication that someone is feeling crushed under the weight of his or her pain or circumstances. Burdens have that effect.

The offenses people feel are easy to objectively identify in strangers—like those people who write angry letters to publications. But when the offended parties are close friends or family members, it gets a lot more complicated. We tend to get sucked into people's issues when they are close to us, and then it's harder to tell whether their perceived offenses are legitimate or not. Before long, we are feeling as weighed down as they are. Bearing one another's burdens is a wonderfully freeing principle when it happens by choice, but it's oppressive and dispiriting when those burdens get dumped on us. The wounds and worries of a dysfunctional family— and all families are at least to some degree dysfunctional— make the unburdened life an enormous challenge.

Just as we can measure people's expectations of us by their degree of offense, we can measure our own expectations of others by how easily we get offended. Our indignation is a symptom of making unreasonable or misplaced assumptions about how people will or should treat us. (I've found, for example, that I get offended at people who get offended too easily. The attitude is very contagious.) When we frequently find ourselves on edge because of the words and actions of other people, we've made inordinate demands on them. Perhaps those demands are subtle or even subconscious, but they are there. We get offended only when someone doesn't meet an expectation we had. When that happens a lot, it's exhausting.

Why do human beings tend to be so easily offended—or pushy, uptight, or unreasonable? Because we're scrambling to get back what we lost in Eden. The identity and security we forfeited in the Fall made us fractured beings and sent us searching for ways to fill all the cracks and holes we suffered by breaking our relationship with God. We began to function out of fear, insecurity, and a deep paranoia that if we don't take care of our interests and our images, no one else will. Our hang-ups are usually manifestations of those pervasive doubts and anxieties. And instead of solving the problem, they make it worse.

Do you see how a life heavy with expectations and offenses can be crippling? Loosening up a little is a much freer way to live. In some people—particularly those with anything-goes, tolerance-is-the-ultimate-virtue belief systems—the laid-back, live-and-let-live philosophy is taken to extremes. But just because there are extremes doesn't mean we should behave in the completely opposite manner. There are aspects of a laid-back approach to life that we could all benefit from.

Determine to be unoffendable. Defensiveness is a heavy burden to bear. Its root is wounded pride, and its fruit is frustration, futility, anger, and stress. But an unoffendable heart suffers no strain. As François Fénelon put it, dead people don't hurt. When we've laid down our own agendas and defused our own pride, neither minor slights nor huge insults can agitate us. We don't respond when we've already laid down our lives as a sacrifice.

> **Determine not to take offense. Defensiveness is a heavy burden to bear.**

The best way to let go of expectations—the ones we have of others and the ones they have of us—is to maintain a Godward focus. With regard to our expectations of others, we have to remember that God is in control and we aren't. He will work through the people around us the way he wants to. With regard to the expectations others have of us, we have to remember that people will place demands on us that God doesn't. We get our instructions from him, not them. He tells us to love and serve others, but that doesn't mean we let them define for us what love and service should look like. When we keep our eyes on him and let him direct us, we will not be overburdened.

Refusing to Pick Them Up

Long after Christian unloaded his burden in *The Pilgrim's Progress*, a different pilgrim asked another character to interpret these enigmatic words: "A man there was, though some did count him mad; the more he gave away, the more he had." The wise man explained the riddle as a principle of giving to the poor. Those who give liberally receive tenfold for their generosity.

Jesus said essentially the same thing to his disciples: "Give, and you will receive. Your gift will return to you in full—pressed down, shaken together to make room for more, running over, and poured into your lap. The amount you give will determine the amount you get back."[7] Though this verse is often used in sermons about stewardship, it was originally spoken in the context of a teaching on love, compassion, and forgiveness. Jesus was making the point that a generous heart receives generous blessings—grace, mercy, giving, etc. This principle applies to every area of life.

That's why Jesus could expect his disciples to turn the other cheek, love their enemies, respond to evil with good, go the extra mile, endure persecution with joy, and so on. People who have already laid down their lives and abandoned their wills to the Father have nothing left to prove and no need to hang on to whatever they think they deserve or even need. They know the Father is taking care of them, and they are able to rest in that. They can give—emotionally, financially, and any other way—because they no longer belong to themselves. They belong to, are supplied by, and are empowered by an inexhaustible source much greater than themselves. The more they give away, the more they have.

In our refusal to pick our burdens back up, we can expect an odd reaction from many of those around us. A lot of people will think we don't care enough or have the compassion we need to have if we don't exhibit extreme stress or panic. In the midst of a crisis, many of those closest to us will expect us to get as worked up as they are—and will have a negative reaction when we don't. That's because active trust in God can sometimes look a lot like passive indifference.

Scripture gives us a couple of examples of this. Jesus was once informed that his good friend Lazarus was about to die, and he intentionally chose not to travel to the scene for two more days. When he finally arrived, Lazarus's sisters pointedly implied that he didn't care enough and should have been there. We've already discussed another occasion in which Jesus slept on a boat during a violent storm while everyone else around him was in an absolute panic. His disciples literally accused him of not caring. But he did care, of course, in spite of their perceptions or his seeming passivity. Trust in God and passive indifference can often look identical on the outside, but they are worlds apart on the inside. When we let go of our stress in troubling situations, we have to also let go of our need for people to understand us.

In our discussion of the difference between a burdened and unburdened life, two distinct portraits have emerged. The burdened personality is preoccupied with achieving personal plans and purposes as well as compensating for emotional wounds. It is also worried about the future, protective of its own ego, defensive, and easily offended. The unburdened personality is unconcerned with personal agendas and trusts God with the future. It is emotionally healthy, humble, unpretentious, and not easily offended. The burdened heart is focused on getting and keeping what it wants and needs; the unburdened one reflects an open-heart and open-hand mentality. In other words, generous people who aren't trying to hang on to what's theirs are able to live in freedom.

> **Generous people who aren't trying to hang on to what's theirs are able to live in freedom.**

Obviously, there are exceptions to these two profiles.

Sometimes we're burdened simply because we have a lot of work to do (although those who are *chronically* overworked may be so for the same dysfunctional reasons the burdened personality normally is). Sometimes we're extremely troubled for people we love and feel the weight of their problems. Sometimes we have a deep desire or strong sense of mission that God has planted in our hearts, and we're passionately concerned about how it will work out. These are normal stressors that are part of the human experience. But when the "exceptions" are a persistent feature of life, a relentless pattern that we can't seem to avoid, then something is most likely wrong. We're probably living with burdens we weren't designed to carry. We have to learn to lay them down.

It's a Decision

The sources of our burdens can be extremely complicated—I've spent a huge portion of this book discussing them and have barely scratched the surface—but the solution for most of them is remarkably simple. We don't have to figure out the root cause of all our wounds and issues in order to deal with them. Neither do we need to analyze every burden and when and how we picked it up. We don't have to understand the reasons we hang on and argue ourselves out of them. The decision to let go is just that: a decision. A choice. A matter of drawing a line for ourselves in the sand and refusing to cross it.

Just because this is simple doesn't mean it's easy, or that it's superficial. We have to be adamant with our own minds and hold out for enduring change. We have to tell ourselves to be humble, not to be defensive, not to be offended and take things personally, not to pose and portray a false image, not to act like we know what we're doing when we don't, and not to push back when we get pushed. If we're sensitive at all to our own tendencies, we'll recognize ourselves doing these things. If we aren't sensitive to our tendencies, we can ask the Holy Spirit to make us so. Regardless of how we become aware of what we're doing, all we need to do is tell ourselves to stop.

The difficulty is in making it a habit. We may have to remind ourselves a hundred times not to be bothered by the person who just cut in front of us in traffic before our reactions finally become natural. We may have to say, "I don't know" a hundred times when we would rather sound intelligent before we're comfortable being honest. We may have to say out loud to ourselves, "I trust you, Lord," again and again before we actually stop worrying. This is the practice of laying burdens down. It requires stubbornness and persistence—and a determination not to keep picking them back up—but eventually they fall off and stay off.

Make a contract with yourself not to do and think the things that bring unnecessary weight to your life. Enforce that decision in your daily, moment-by-moment choices. Whenever you start to feel the need to maneuver and manage, remind yourself that it's unnecessary and resist it. Whenever the burdens you cling to threaten your peace, just let go.

CHAPTER 6

PASSION

IMAGINE YOUR FIRST day in heaven. All of your problems, all of your stresses, all of your best-laid plans for your life are over. There will be no more personal strategizing, no more late-night anxiety, no more pressure to pay the bills on time or save your children from horrendous mistakes or deal with the dysfunction of the people around you. You'll have no sense of incompleteness or longing that can't be fulfilled. All of your deepest hungers and thirsts have either become immediately irrelevant and powerless, or they have been realized with the best possible fulfillment you could have imagined. You'll never fear anything again, you'll never worry again, and you'll never grieve or suffer disappointment.

Instead, you have a deep-seated sense that you'll never have another need again. You walk around in amazement at the sights you're seeing and the people and other beings you meet. You have complete freedom to feel joy and be confident of the victorious atmosphere that surrounds you. You may have work to do—Scripture gives us no indication that we'll be inactive in heaven—but it will be satisfying work that causes no stress. You can freely soak in the wonder and excitement and adventure of where you are. You are completely whole and fully at peace. The whole experience makes you feel as light as a feather.

In a very real sense, that's the cross and resurrection we've already been baptized into. When we come to Christ, we lay everything down at his feet—not just our treasures and pleasures, but also our problems and pains. Then we're raised up in new life. That's what Paul meant when he wrote that he was crucified with Christ, that he no longer lived but Jesus lived in him;[1] and when he wrote that "we died and were buried with Christ by baptism. And just as Christ was raised from the dead by the glorious power of the Father, now we also may live new lives."[2]

Most people sense a clean break with certain attitudes and ways of life when they are converted, but experiencing a clean break with past circumstances is much more rare. A lot of situations from our pre-Christian lives carry over into our Christian lives. That's why we don't sense the freedom we will feel on our first day in heaven. We still know the same people, have the same families, experience the same situations and problems, manage the same issues, and get the same bills. We still have to deal with life in a fallen world.

Even so, the gospel promises us a fresh start—actually, a bunch of them. We always have the option of laying down certain attitudes and behaviors and picking up new ones. That's a process much longer and more involved than dying and waking up in heaven, but it's supposed to be the same dynamic. There's no reason we can't bring the attitudes of heaven into our earthly experience. We have every reason to look forward to the reality of God's Kingdom and live with Kingdom perspectives now.

This is, in fact, what Scripture urges us to do:

> *Even when he reached the land God promised him, [Abraham] lived there by faith—for he was like a foreigner, living in tents. And so did Isaac and Jacob, who inherited the same promise. Abraham was confidently looking forward to a city with eternal foundations, a city designed and built by God.[3]*

> *Since you have been raised to new life with Christ, set your sights on the realities of heaven, where Christ sits in the place of honor at God's right hand. Think about the things of heaven, not the things of earth. For you died to this life, and your real life is hidden with Christ in God. And when Christ, who is your life, is revealed to the whole world, you will share in all his glory.[4]*

We don't look at the troubles we can see now; rather, we fix our gaze on things that cannot be seen. For the things we see now will soon be gone, but the things we cannot see will last forever.[5]

These are only a few of many examples of how we should think while we live in this world. A heavenly perspective is an integral part of the unburdened life.

The One Thing

People don't erase a whiteboard in order for it to remain clean. They don't declare bankruptcy in order never to buy anything again. And they don't raze a building on prime real estate in order to leave the lot empty. Any intentional finish or clean slate is for the purpose of starting something new.

A heavenly perspective is an integral part of the unburdened life.

Likewise, we don't die with Christ in order to be dead. We choose to let go of our burdens not so we can sit on the couch and do nothing but so we can do what we were meant to do and live the way we were meant to live. We lay down our lives in order to be raised up to new life. That new life will be filled with a lot of the same circumstances and people we faced in the old one. So what exactly is new about it? What aspect of our new state is supposed to be more liberating than the way of life we used to know?

There are several answers to these questions, not the least of which is the empowerment we get from the Spirit within us. But one reason the new, unburdened life is so different from the old, heavy-laden life is the different focus we have. Like the man who found a treasure in a field and sold all he had to buy that field,[6] we trade in a complicated web of multifaceted focal points for one overriding passion. We shift from people who are focused on relationships and bills and plans and desires and clothes and food and housing and retirement to people who serve Jesus. That simplifies life a lot.

A well-known scene from the movie *City Slickers* amusingly illustrates this principle. Curly, the salty old rancher who is guiding the three city slickers on a cattle drive, offers to tell Mitch (Billy Crystal) the secret of life. He holds up one finger and says, "One thing. Just one thing. You stick to that, and the rest don't mean [garbage]." When Mitch presses him to explain what the "one thing" is, Curly smiles and tells him, "That's what *you* have to find out."[7]

Mitch thinks this cryptic advice is pointing to one big secret that Curly won't reveal, and when Curly dies soon afterward, Mitch thinks the secret has died with him. But by the end of the movie, he figures it out. Curly never intended to specify what the one thing was; he was simply saying that a single exclusive focus is the key to success. For Curly, it was cattle ranching. That's all he did, and he did it well. For Mitch and the other two city slickers, it could be anything else. The point was to live life with one priority and not with a scattered, diversified soul.

This movie scene echoes the theme of a 1929 novel by Lloyd C. Douglas, *The Magnificent Obsession*, in which a surgeon receives a journal from his mentor that explains the secret to success. That secret, the only way to be truly fulfilled, is to quietly and sacrificially serve people in need. Douglas is said to have based his novel on Matthew 6:1-4, a passage in which Jesus urges his disciples to practice their righteousness secretly and not before men. The phrase "magnificent obsession" has been used in evangelical circles since then as a description of exclusive devotion to Jesus.

It's significant that one of the key verses in a passage about worry—the section in the Sermon on the Mount in which Jesus tells his disciples to look to the birds and the flowers as role models[8]—offers this viable alternative. Not only are we taught not to focus on food and clothes and the worries of life, we're told which overarching priority we *should* focus on: "Seek first his kingdom and his righteousness, and all these things will be given to you as well."[9]

Anyone who has tried to eliminate worry and stress from his or her life by focusing on the worry and stress has fought a futile battle. It isn't enough to lay all our burdens down. That never works. It's a right and necessary start, but it isn't the whole picture. When we "let go," we leave a void, and it's our nature to fill the vacuum with something. We can't just let go and not grab on to anything; if we did, we would have empty, pointless lives. No, the answer is to replace what we've let go of with something else. Jesus tells us what the proper replacement is: a magnificent obsession with the Kingdom of God.

This principle applies to many areas of life, both mundane and spiritually crucial. It's virtually impossible, for example, to get one persistent tune out of your head without first replacing it with another. It's hard to get over one lost love without finding a new one. We don't cease from sin by trying to eliminate it, but by living instead by the Spirit.[10] So it only makes sense that we get rid of our burdens not by focusing on them but by

> When we "let go," we leave a void, and it's our nature to fill the vacuum with something.

finding a much more worthy replacement. This replacement is heavier, in the sense that it's much more important than anything we've clung to before; but it's also much lighter, in the sense that we aren't really the ones who have to handle the weight of it. When God's Kingdom—including his presence, his character, and his ways—is our singular obsession, we find supernatural strength supporting us.

Letting Go and Picking Up

The book of Philippians is a virtual case study in how to let go of weighty burdens and pick up the much bigger but lighter burden God gives us. From what we know of the book, circumstances aren't making life easy either for Paul or the Philippians. Paul is apparently writing to this church during his two-year (or longer) custody in Rome, an open-ended term of house arrest during which he has been responsible for all of his own expenses. He can't be employed during this time, so he has no income, but he has to fund the apartment he and his guard live in and the food they eat. While many Christians assume that Paul's arrest has been a blow to the spread of the gospel, some of his rivals seem to see it as an opportunity to make a name for themselves. In trying to establish their own ministries, they've created a culture of competition. They build up their own reputations and develop communities that support their own pet doctrines— and Paul has no choice but to sit on the sidelines and listen to reports about them. The normally active, hands-on apostle must watch while Kingdom work that fills his heart is being done by others.

Meanwhile, Paul isn't sure how his trial is going to turn out. Rome's leaders haven't yet reacted all that strongly to the kind of religious "crimes" he has allegedly committed, but at this point in history, emperors seem to be increasingly unpredictable. Is he going to be released or held indefinitely? Is he going to live or die? He doesn't know. It could go either way.

Sitting in an apartment in Rome, Paul has had plenty of time to think about the events that got him into his predicament. He went to Jerusalem against the prophetic advice of many, and persecution erupted just as he and his friends had expected. But two years in prison there, plus two more in Rome, is enough to make even an apostle worry about how long he has been out of commission. There are hurting churches to comfort, new churches to establish, and lots of conflicts to resolve. Is house arrest really the best way to spend his time? Has God sidelined him for a reason? Has he offended the Father? Are the opponents who continue to slander him being vindicated by God?

While under house arrest, the Philippians send Paul some money and reports of how the congregation is faring. But their messenger, Epaphroditus, falls sick while in Rome and must be taken care of by Paul's companions, who include Timothy and possibly Luke—but few others, if any at all. Churches in Rome have apparently not rallied around Paul. He considers himself virtually alone.

What will Paul tell these Philippians who have sent letters of comfort and asked for his advice? Life isn't easy for them either. They have been faithful, but factions have risen up within their fellowship. Two influential women are at odds with each other and are undermining the once-solid unity of the congregation. The ever-present threat of false teachers seems to have become more than just a threat. "Dogs" are leading Gentile Christians away from the simplicity of the gospel and putting legalistic burdens on them. The believers' faith is being undermined by contradictory doctrines, internal division, a former leader's imprisonment, and anxiety about all of the above. The situation isn't critical yet—this is still a strong church—but the seeds of crisis have already been sown. If the Jesus movement is threatened in Philippi, it can be threatened anywhere.

At this critical moment in his life, Paul has plenty of opportunities to question God, worry about his circumstances, be anxious for his future, mistrust the hand that guides him, try to prove himself, defend his rights, and assert his authority. From one perspective, it seems that the Kingdom is passing him by. Truth twisters across the empire are undoing much of the work he has risked his life for. He has been beaten and stoned more times than he wants to remember, he has been shipwrecked and bitten by a snake, and he has worked ceaselessly for his magnificent obsession. Now he is being maligned by many outside of the church (and even quite a few within it), and he is tied up in the Roman legal system and facing the possibility of execution.

Many of us in such circumstances would feel crushed under the weight of them. We would wonder where we went wrong, try to compensate for all our failures, lie awake at night wondering how things were going to turn out, feel guilty for all the people we may have let down or offended or even led astray, second-guess all the decisions of our pasts, and ask "what if" about all the possibilities of our futures. Paul's circumstances were the perfect environment to cultivate the burdened life.

> **Paul's circumstances were the perfect environment to cultivate the burdened life.**

We know, of course, that Paul's letter to the Philippians is filled with words of joy and peace and encouragement. There are no overbearing burdens in this letter, no words of defeat or despair, and no tears of regret. In fact, we can see just the opposite. All of the characteristics of an unburdened life are on display in this letter.

What does Paul say about his imprisonment, for example? God is actually using his confinement to spread the gospel in influential places—throughout the praetorian guard and in Caesar's courts. In spite of the ways his rivals are capitalizing on his predicament, the gospel is being preached with greater zeal than before—with selfish motives, lamentably, but still with greater exposure. And the potential end-game scenario for his imprisonment is a win-win situation. If he lives, he will be able to continue to "be" Christ in a needy world and among his churches. If not . . . well, that will be even better. A tired, sore body has nothing to lose by going to be with Jesus. Either way is fine with Paul.

Throughout the first chapter of the letter, Paul demonstrates the characteristics he will soon urge the Philippians to adopt for themselves: humility in the face of proud, self-centered people; a refusal to defend his reputation; a complete lack of worry about the situation he's in; and extremely loose expectations about how he will be treated in the future. There's a lot of trust in his words and, as a result, a sense of absolute freedom.

Twice in the letter, Paul urges his readers to remember that they are citizens of heaven and should have a heavenly perspective.[11] The backbone of his letter is a landmark passage about humility and servanthood.[12] There's no attempt to resist the fact that he is being poured out like a liquid offering;[13] it's natural for a Kingdom-oriented servant of God to let go of his life. Paul overflows with passion about his magnificent obsession—how he considers everything "worthless when compared with the infinite value of knowing Christ Jesus"[14] and, putting the past behind him, determines to "focus on this one thing."[15] In fact, Paul is so at ease in his circumstances that he can urge the Philippians to

- rejoice in an attitude of worship,[16]
- embrace selflessness,[17]
- refuse to worry and choose to trust God,[18]
- replace their anxious thoughts with the Kingdom-first perspectives of whatever is pure and true and right,[19]
- consider him an example of living with loose expectations,[20]
- be empowered by the supernatural strength within them,[21]
- and trust God in all situations.[22]

From beginning to end, Paul's words to the Philippian church are a recipe for the unburdened life.

It's no coincidence that the liberating attitudes we've discussed as keys to the unburdened life are thoroughly reflected in one of the most joyful portions of Scripture. It's also no coincidence that the overriding characteristic of this free, unburdened servant of God is his singular passion for the things of the Kingdom. We see clearly in Paul not only that he has let go of his pride, his reputation, his personal agendas, and his anxieties, but that he has picked up the one enormous but weightless burden of loving and serving Jesus alone. Paul could be distressed by the many threats to his security and the welfare of the Philippian church, but he isn't. He's obsessed with the Kingdom of God. And he can see that at work in any situation, no matter how negative the situation appears to others.

We should be clear that none of Paul's issues went away simply because he refused to be worried by them. He was still confined, financially strapped, aware of people's problems, and uncertain about his future. He was genuinely concerned for Epaphroditus and for the Philippians. He was truly bothered by false teachers who undermined the gospel. No aspect of his environment changed immediately by his attitude. But his attitude made all the difference in how he handled his environment. There's a lightness to the Philippian letter that we wish we had and, according to Paul's reassuring words, that we *can* have.

How did Paul arrive at his apparent weightlessness? He trusted God implicitly, for one thing, but because of his trust he also did what we've discussed in the last two chapters: he let go of the many concerns and reattached himself to one. The result was a heart free from anxiety and full of joy and peace.

Worthless Loss and Priceless Gain

When I think of Paul's passion for the gospel—and really the attitude we should all have toward God's Kingdom—I envision a guy walking on a long, arduous journey through the mountains and suddenly, unexpectedly, getting a glimpse of some shiny, dazzling reflections through a small opening in a wall of rock. Turning aside to investigate more closely, he can tell that the glow is coming from a stash of jewels and precious metals. As he looks into the crevice, he sees not only the brilliant glimmering of the treasures that first caught his eye but also a vast, opulent city spreading out into what looks like a whole other world. And everything in him wants to enter.

The problem is that the opening is so small that only the traveler's body can squeeze through it. He will have to leave his pack—filled with all of his necessary supplies and the valuable keepsakes that remind him of home—behind. And any treasure he picks up from inside will have to remain inside; he can't bring it back out into the world he came from. But from the looks of what he has seen, he wouldn't want to come back anyway. In his mind, this will be a one-way trip.

What would a traveler in that frame of mind do? Given the choice between holding on to an old, heavy backpack and starting fresh in a new but lavish Kingdom with nothing but the clothes on his back, it seems obvious. Who wouldn't leave the burden behind? But some of us are so attached to what we've carried for so long that the idea of setting it down and walking away makes us very uncomfortable. And the idea of picking up a new treasure to carry instead, with the promise that this one is lighter and much easier to manage, is scary simply because of all the unknown variables involved. What if the treasure doesn't satisfy us? What if it's heavier than it looks? What if we've been promised a magnificent obsession that we won't be all that wild about once we get a closer look?

Exchanging the known for the unknown can be a frightening proposition, even when we are thoroughly unsatisfied with the known.

This is where that issue of trust comes into play again. The only way to live an unburdened life—the one take-it-or-leave-it, all-or-nothing way—is to actually let go of what we've been carrying *and* pick up a singular passion for God. We can't just let go. That doesn't work because we *will* pick something back up. We can't let go and then pick up a passion for God-plus-other-treasures. We have to make this exchange thoroughly and decisively. We let go *and* refocus on the "one thing," knowing that the one thing brings the supernatural strength and freedom of God into our lives.

> The only way to live an unburdened life—the one, take-it-or-leave-it, all-or-nothing way—is to actually let go of what we've been carrying *and* pick up a singular passion for God.

Paul is a great example of what this looks like. His life before Christ was filled with a personal agenda strong enough to kill people who threatened it, pride in his long-cultivated pedigree, and the righteousness that comes from human effort. His own description of his former life practically oozes with heavy burdens:

> *I could have confidence in my own effort if anyone could.*
> *Indeed, if others have reason for confidence in their own*

efforts, I have even more! I was circumcised when I was eight days old. I am a pure-blooded citizen of Israel and a member of the tribe of Benjamin—a real Hebrew if there ever was one! I was a member of the Pharisees, who demand the strictest obedience to the Jewish law. I was so zealous that I harshly persecuted the church. And as for righteousness, I obeyed the law without fault.[23]

But then he clearly spells out that he not only let his entire past go—i.e., he dumped the backpack at the entrance to the new Kingdom—but he picked up a much more worthy substitute.

I once thought these things were valuable, but now I consider them worthless because of what Christ has done. Yes, everything else is worthless when compared with the infinite value of knowing Christ Jesus my Lord. For his sake I have discarded everything else, counting it all as garbage, so that I could gain Christ and become one with him.[24]

How does that work for Paul? Well, think about how he reacts to people before he meets Jesus on the Damascus road. We may get a glimpse of this at the end of Acts 6. Stephen and six other men—all Hellenistic Jews (i.e., Jews not from Palestine), from what their names and assignments tell us—have been appointed to oversee the distribution of food so that Greek-speaking widows get their fair share.[25] But in the very next passage, Stephen is drawn into a debate among members of the Synagogue of Freed Slaves, a community of Jews who have come from other parts of the empire but are living in Jerusalem. Among its members are Cilicians—people from Paul's home territory, including Tarsus.[26] This is where Paul would most naturally worship every Sabbath.

We don't know for sure that Paul is one of the key debaters who argues (unsuccessfully) with Stephen, but it's easy to imagine the belligerence that Stephen's words would stir up in Paul. What we do know for certain is that Paul is the one overseeing Stephen's mob execution in the next chapter. His contentiousness isn't just a momentary defense of his version of truth, it is a lifestyle. It has to be if it leads to such extremes.

Fast-forward to Paul's first visit to Philippi. After some time of ministry there, Paul and Silas are dragged into the marketplace by angry owners of a slave girl from whom Paul has cast out a demon. The owners have lost their fortune-teller, and they are able to stir up a mob against these unwelcome Jews. The local magistrates feel it necessary to appease the crowd, so they strip Paul and Silas and have them beaten the way Romans normally beat people—with bruising, bone-breaking rods. Then they stick them in a prison cell and put their feet in stocks designed for extreme discomfort.

If the old Paul is ever going to show up again, this is a likely moment. But the new Paul never claims his status as a Roman citizen during his beating, which would end the illegal punishment immediately, and he and Silas begin singing hymns while bound in their cell. Paul does not seem outraged that someone of his pedigree is being treated so harshly, he doesn't seem stressed that his agenda for ministry in Philippi is being threatened, he doesn't seem worried that God has lost control of the situation, and he doesn't even seize the opportunity to escape when God provides a propitious earthquake. The anxiety that normally plagues us in threatening circumstances was noticeably absent. Why? Because Paul's only objective is the Kingdom of God—not his defense or his agenda—and he seems to know that this turn of events is ordained by the God who is zealous for his Kingdom. He is free to trust and go with the flow.

That's what the unburdened life should look like for us, too. We are free to trust God and go with the flow. That doesn't mean that we won't have any concerns, that we'll never need to defend ourselves, that we'll never get into an argument, and that we'll never think about the future again—Paul did all these things and more long after his conversion, as is evident from Acts and his letters. He defended the truth, his own apostleship, and his churches. But he wasn't consumed with these things. He wasn't worried to the point of being weighed down with life. He urged the Philippians to rejoice and the Thessalonians to give thanks in everything.[27] He moved through obstacles and challenges with confidence and trust, without being hampered or even overly distracted by them. We can too.

If you're wondering how this translates to your life, think about what fills your thoughts when you lie down to go to sleep at night, when you wake up in the morning, and in your other mental "downtime." Whatever you're preoccupied with is a high priority to you. Now what would it take to feel unburdened by that priority? You would have to choose to trust God about it, for one thing, but how would that priority look if it placed a distant second to the higher priority of doing whatever God wants at any moment of any day? If your thoughts were consumed with pursuing God and his presence and his Kingdom, how heavy would threats to lesser priorities seem? The point is that we are always most weighed down by our highest priority, and if our highest priority is supported and upheld by God himself, then all of our fears and worries suddenly seem a lot smaller.

That doesn't mean we won't ever be anxious for our children's welfare or wonder how we're going to pay the bills. It does mean, however, that even such personal concerns take a backseat in our lives to the bigger issues. I believe that's what Jesus has in mind when he tells his disciples, "If you want to be my disciple, you must hate everyone else by comparison—your father and mother, wife and children, brothers and sisters—yes, even your own life. Otherwise, you cannot be my disciple. And if you do not carry your own cross and follow me, you cannot be my disciple."[28] Maybe that's the hard demand we normally read it as, but I think it's more of an invitation to let go of the things that crush us and be consumed with the one thing that won't. Like Jesus, we need to be able to say, "My nourishment comes from doing the will of God, who sent me, and from finishing his work."[29]

When we breathe his desires and crave his will, that's single-minded freedom.

There's a huge difference between concern and worry. When we've let go of our burdens and picked up a passion for the Kingdom, we'll still be concerned for the people and issues God has put in our hands. But we won't be worried about them. We'll be free from the stress of having to know that they will behave or work out in the way we want them to. We'll experience the joy and the peace of a better Kingdom.

Jesus' command that we carry our cross and follow him is an invitation to let go of the things that crush us and be consumed with the one thing that won't.

CHAPTER 7

PERSPECTIVE

A FRIEND SENT me a link to a video clip that illustrated the power of perspective better than any sermon illustration I've heard. It featured a comedian, Louis C.K., on a late-night talk show talking about how "everything is amazing right now, and nobody's happy." For example, we used to have to stand next to a phone attached to a wall and use a rotary device to dial numbers. At the time, this was a technological feat. Now it seems prehistoric—so primitive that when we don't get a signal on our cell phones in a matter of a few seconds, we get agitated at the inconvenience. "Give it a second," the comedian yelled. "It's going to space!" He pointed out that we get upset when a flight is delayed and we have to sit on a runway for forty whole minutes—even though it used to take years to get from coast to coast, with babies being born and people dying along the way. Now it takes five hours to get from New York to Los Angeles, and our perspective has changed. "You're sitting in a chair . . . in the *sky!*" Louis reminded the audience. And yet we complain about how the seat doesn't go back more than a couple of inches while we're enjoying the mind-boggling miracle of flight.[1]

Besides being funny, the comedian's remarks were very insightful. To an enormous degree, our perspectives determine how content we are and how burdened we feel. When we're used to instant access to information, it's terribly frustrating for a Web page to take ten seconds to open. Yet that single page contains more information than a league of medieval town criers could have disseminated across a single region in a week's time. If we lived in the Middle Ages, we would be grateful for news that got to us within a matter of days. At this point in the technological revolution, news is excruciatingly slow if we don't get it in a few seconds, and ridiculously out of date in a matter of days. What's the difference? Perspective.

Much of the weightiness of life depends on the lens we look through. When I've just come back from vacation, I dread going into the office for an eight-hour day. But when I've been under enormous pressure to finish a book manuscript on deadline, staying up past midnight for weeks just to get the work done, an eight-hour day looks like a walk in the park. When I get the flu and have to stay in bed for a few days, I'm terribly frustrated at the discomfort and the waste of time. But if I had ever survived a three-year bout with cancer and chemo, I'd be deeply grateful that I was now having to spend only a week in bed with the flu. If my kids had always been well-behaved and then were caught skipping class, I'd be extremely upset. If they had been in trouble with the law repeatedly over the last few years, skipping class would be a minor issue. In each of these situations, the burden I felt would be related to the context in which I experienced it.

That's how perspective works. Your problems and issues look the way they do to you because of where you sit. Under different circumstances or at different times, they might not carry the same weight. And if that's true, then it must be possible to lighten our loads by changing the way we view them.

The process we've talked about so far—letting go of burdens and picking up an obsession for God—will do a lot to change our perspectives without any specific effort to do so on our parts. But there's more we can do to keep reminding ourselves where the loads we carry fit into the grand scheme of things. If we can (1) be aware of our perspectives and (2) reposition them, we can affect our outlooks and potentially the sense of freedom we have.

I've found that there are a few key kinds of perspective that shape how I look at life. This is by no means an exhaustive list—you may realize other areas that apply to you—but I believe those who are at least aware of these basic angles have the tools to radically change how they perceive the world, themselves, and God.

Time

I remember going through one of life's painful seasons a few years ago and wondering, *When will it all end?* It seemed unreasonable to me that God would allow certain circumstances to be so prolonged. I was discouraged, depressed, and weighed down for several years. I felt like I was being crushed, and there was no end in sight.

During one of my many laments to God in this season, I was hit with the thought that even if I suffered painfully for the rest of my life, it would still be a short time. I'd been struggling with the feeling that five years seemed like an eternity, and yet eternity lay before me with an emphatic promise that my troubles would be ending forever at some point. When I looked ahead at the next decade of my life, I grew discouraged. When I looked ahead to my millions and billions of years in the Kingdom of God—as if the Kingdom even functions in "years"—the outlook on my next decade seemed as threatening as a mosquito on a summer's eve: annoying but hardly worth getting worked up about.

That shift in perspective didn't make my difficult circumstances go away. It did, however, make them much easier to bear. Since then, I've had to remind myself several times of the difference between time and eternity. It's easy to define "life" as the next several decades until we die rather than an open-ended adventure with God that only begins in this age. That's why we spend most of our time planning for things like careers, financial security, and all the provisions and comforts we need while, at times, neglecting the things that last forever. We think of "life" as a very temporary commodity.

But that isn't how the Bible defines life. We who are redeemed by God are living in our earthly bodies for a limited time, during which we will suffer persecution and pain. If those few years were the whole story, we would have every reason to get discouraged. Or, as Paul put it, "if our hope in Christ is only for this life, we are more to be pitied than anyone in the world."[2] The reason we can have a positive outlook on the future is that no matter how bad things get, no matter how long we think they are going to last, the extent of our lives in our mortal bodies is a tiny, tiny fraction of even a small slice of a momentary fragment of eternity.

In studying the life of Abraham recently, I felt very offended at how God dealt with him. I, too, have waited a long time for God to fulfill some promises, and I know how frustrating and painful that wait can be. But twenty-five years? Giving a man a promise at the age of seventy-five and then intentionally not fulfilling it until he's one hundred? I would be almost past the point of caring by the time God got around to doing what he said. If God waits until I'm an old man to fulfill certain promises he has given me, there will be times when I wonder whether the promises are worth the wait. But when you're waiting on God for a miracle, you don't have the choice of *not* waiting. You can't rush his miracles and make them come sooner. He does them when he does them.

You can, however, see his promises in the grand scheme of eternity and let that perspective shape your attitude.

Apparently that's what Abraham did. He "was confidently looking forward to a city with eternal foundations."[3] He fixed his eyes on the big picture and, according to Paul, "never wavered in believing."[4] He looked ahead and knew that the future according to God is unimaginably vast, and his trials and long wait were momentary.

I believe in the immediate implications of the statement that "no eye has seen, no ear has heard, and no mind has imagined what God has prepared for those who love him."[5] But if this statement has implications for this age, how much more does it apply to the eternity set before us? There will be nothing stagnant or stale about the new earth or heaven, and every aspect of it is good for those who have loved God and been redeemed by his Son. However our perspectives are interpreting our current circumstances, we're still seeing them as disproportionately large. There will come a time when our worst afflictions in this life are a faint, distant memory.

> **See God's promises in the grand scheme of eternity and let that perspective shape your attitude.**

We get glimpses of this even in our current states. I can remember a time in high school when I could certainly understand people with suicidal tendencies. I was depressed about a number of problems in school and in my social life, and I had magnified them to the degree that I thought they were surely permanent. I assumed I would *always* be frustrated and lonely and depressed. That's how things appear when you see no way out. Your current snapshot of life looks like a portrait of how it will always be. Now, quite a few years later, I can hardly remember the circumstances that were weighing me down. That whole season of discouragement seems like a blip on the screen of life.

If we transfer that dynamic to a much larger scope, we can imagine a day when we'll look back on the painful trials of life—or even the entirety of our lives in these bodies—as a blip on the screen of our eternal existence. I believe that's what Paul had in mind when he wrote about our "light and momentary troubles" working toward an eternal glory in which the benefits far outweigh the costs.[6] Light and momentary? Is he kidding? He has just written about carrying around the death of Jesus in his body—of being hard-pressed but not crushed, perplexed but not desperate, persecuted but not abandoned, struck down but not destroyed. He has written elsewhere of his many beatings, stonings, imprisonments, adversaries, and more. Yet all of these things are light and momentary, a brief blip on the screen of his eternal life, a tiny burden compared to the weight of glory to come. The only way he could possibly think such a thing was by seeing "life" as an eternal adventure, not as a several-decade event.

Values

By implication, our perspectives in the area of our values change pretty dramatically when we've traded in our many concerns for an overarching obsession with God. He *is* our highest value. The things of his Kingdom mean more to us than they used to mean. But for those times when we start to worry about the temporal cares Jesus told us not to worry about, it's good to ask ourselves what we really value.

This issue came up in Jesus' ministry from time to time. The well-known character we refer to as "the rich young ruler" came to Jesus asking how to inherit eternal life; somehow he seemed to know that keeping the commandments wasn't enough. Jesus targeted his value system. Did he love his possessions more than he loved God? Was he more interested in his lifestyle or the eternal Kingdom? Was he willing to lose himself in order to find himself? To lay it all down in order to pick up something better?

No, he wasn't. His values were skewed. He went away sad because he treasured lesser riches more than he treasured truth. And in his wake, Jesus made a statement that shocked his disciples: the wealthy—those who seem so clearly blessed by God—have a really hard time entering God's rest. In fact, it's easier for a camel to go through the eye of a needle than for a rich man to enter the Kingdom.[7]

I'd venture to say that it's also easier for a camel to go through the eye of a needle than for a person with skewed values to find peace and rest in this life. An old Sunday school illustration asserts that there really was an entrance to Jerusalem (or any other city in Palestine) called "the eye of the needle" that one could enter only if he dismounted his camel and stripped the beast of all its other burdens. There's not a shred of evidence for this illustration, but it's a great picture of shedding extra baggage—much like my hypothetical traveler in the last chapter having to enter an extravagantly wealthy city through a crack in a rock wall. We can apply these word pictures not only to the possessions we own but to any of our misplaced values. If we are unwilling to unload the things we hold dear, we can't experience the freedom God wants us to experience.

A man once brought a legal dispute to Jesus and asked him to render a decision. The issue was an inheritance—a vital issue in God's law—yet Jesus deflected the responsibility to act as an arbiter. Then he followed up his deferral with a pointed parable about values. He told how a man focused on establishing his own security by building bigger and better barns, amassing more wealth, and pursuing a life of comfort and pleasure—a picture not far removed from the American dream. Jesus called this man a fool. Not a man with slightly misplaced values, not a man who needed gentle but firm correction, but a fool. "Yes, a person is a fool to store up earthly wealth but not have a rich relationship with God."[8]

The irony of this parable is that the man who sought to build up his wealth was seeking a state of rest—and actually could have reached his goal temporarily. But as with virtually anyone who seeks to build an earthly kingdom and enjoy its pleasures, the costs always outweigh the benefits. This is the pursuit that keeps us always seeking but never really finding, always running but never arriving, always chasing the wind but never finding anything meaningful. The pursuit itself creates all kinds of burdens for us that a simple quest for God and his Kingdom would never impose on us. When we see our lives as missions to achieve a certain lifestyle or acquire a certain amount, we will either be frustrated by failure or disappointed by how unfulfilling success can be. Neither is an outcome of a passionate pursuit of God. Valuing him above all results in peace and rest; valuing anything else above him results in stress and frustration. When our perspectives cause us to see people, things, or experiences as central and God as peripheral, we're bound to end up burdened.

> When our perspectives cause us to see people, things, or experiences as central and God as peripheral, we're bound to end up burdened.

Outlook

Some people see the glass as half empty; others see it as half full. Well, that's the theory. In my experience, it takes about 90 percent of fullness and about 10 percent of emptiness for most people to see "half and half." We have a tendency to focus on what's lacking in our lives, what needs to be different in order for us to be fully content. The result is a perception that we are constantly missing out.

I've found this false perspective particularly frustrating and hard to overcome. I can be blessed with good health, three tasty meals a day, a warm and comfortable home, a fantastic job, plenty of modern conveniences, and lots of people who love me, and still be absolutely despondent over a plan that didn't work out or a goal I didn't meet. I've known people who felt horribly disadvantaged because they couldn't buy the car they wanted, take the vacation they dreamed of, or get the job they were after—even though they had a great car, took nice vacations, and enjoyed the job they already had. There's something about fallen human nature that dismisses blessings almost as soon as we get them and stews about the missed opportunities we think we might have been able to take advantage of if we'd only had the chance. We can catch a thousand proverbial fish and be consumed with bitterness over the one that got away.

I've noticed this tendency not only in myself but also in my kids. They have an ongoing wish list—we call it a Christmas list in December, but it's actually a year-round reality—that is always topped by something they absolutely, positively have to have. Then when they get that much-coveted item, they play with it for a couple of days and then start thinking about what they absolutely, positively have to have next. There's very little time to enjoy the moment before moving on to the next thing. When we have this perspective as children, the stakes aren't very high. But when it translates into adulthood, it keeps us moving from house to house, city to city, job to job, or even spouse to spouse. It never lets us rest.

This negative outlook—i.e., a perspective that focuses on lack—has the power to undermine our present happiness and to set us up for future disappointment. It steals the current moment from us by causing us to forget how greatly we've been blessed, but it also virtually assures us that we won't be satisfied with how things turn out. When our expectations are detailed and rigid, we're bound to be disenchanted with some aspect of the future that doesn't turn out right. We can't enjoy our situations, the detours God takes us on, the surprises he brings into our lives, or the people who invariably don't behave according to our exact predictions. With this outlook, we find a way to be dissatisfied.

> **We can catch a thousand proverbial fish and be consumed with bitterness over the one that got away.**

It's easy to see the problem with this perspective. It's a slave driver. It pushes us relentlessly but never gives us any pleasure. It magnifies the worst aspects of our lives and minimizes the many, many ways we've been blessed.

Self

Jesus told a story about a proud Pharisee and a dishonest tax collector who went to the Temple to pray. The Pharisee thanked God for his own righteousness, while the tax collector beat himself up for his sinfulness and begged for mercy. Jesus declared the sinner justified and held him up as an example.

That's a great picture of how we come into the Kingdom and of the humility we are supposed to have before God.

But a lot of Christians never get past the self-deprecating stage and realize who they are in Christ. The same Savior who honored the humility of the tax collector also said he would share his glory with his followers and prayed that they would be as united to him as he was to the Father.[9] We are told that we are seated with the exalted Savior in heaven,[10] that we are royal priests,[11] and that we will rule with him.[12] These are lofty words for those who came into the Kingdom as completely unworthy miscreants. We are the ultimate rags-to-riches story.

Why does this matter? Because our perspective of ourselves has a huge effect on how we live and, more specifically, on the burdens we bear. When we see ourselves primarily as sinners who have been redeemed, we tend to play the part. We focus more on the sinful nature that we can't seem to shake, and the more we verbally or mentally build it up, the more power it has over us. The result is a constant sense of failing God and an inability to grow in purity and holiness. We receive God's mercy and keep trying to overcome our sinful selves, but we keep failing. That's because we are *sinners* who have been saved. It's still our perceived identity.

When we see ourselves as chosen and holy children of God, born of his own substance and nature, we tend to play that part instead. We're aware that we aren't immune to sin, of course, and we certainly don't have any proud illusion that we overcame sin ourselves, but if we know we're completely surrounded by grace and have a righteous Spirit freely living within us, we behave accordingly. As a result, we live without a sense of guilt and shame, even when we trip up every once in a while.

I believe this is why Paul emphasized that if we live by the Spirit, we won't carry out the deeds of the flesh.[13] Scripture never tells us to overcome our sin by targeting our sinfulness. That's a losing battle from the start. That's the principle behind Paul's teaching that we should consider ourselves dead to sin but alive to God.[14] "Considering" ourselves to be who God says we are is another way of saying "make this your perspective." We're to focus on our true identity in Jesus.

Many of us are a lot like a street kid in a third-world country who has been adopted by the richest family in town. You can take an orphan out of the street culture, but it's a lot harder to get the street culture out of the orphan. How long does it take for an adopted vagabond to stop hoarding food at one meal because he isn't sure he'll be invited to the table again for the next one? Or to stop pocketing trinkets from the household because it hasn't sunk in that the entire estate is his as a member of the family? Or to stop giving his adoptive parents a nod and a handshake when he sees them because he doesn't trust their hugs? Or to stop asking permission to do basic things like sit on the couch or watch TV? The point is that being at home in God's Kingdom implies a whole different attitude than we would have as barely welcome visitors. Only one of those mind-sets allows us to relax.

Seeing ourselves as sinners who have been saved rather than saints who sometimes sin may seem subtle, but it makes a huge difference. One is a negative focus that results in futility and an unbearable weight, and the other is a positive focus that leads to freedom. And the positive approach actually does a better job of accomplishing what our negative approach tried to do. Those who see themselves as adopted children of God in whom he absolutely delights find themselves growing in purity in ways that a person focused on his utter need for mercy never does. In the arena of our all-important relationship with God, one perspective brings life and liberty while the other brings backbreaking frustration.

Our focus on overcoming sin points to a larger issue related to our perspectives of ourselves: the tendency to focus on self in the first place. I strongly believe, mainly because I've seen it in my own life, that an inward focus gradually increases our burdens, anxieties, and fears, while an outward focus on God and others gradually decreases them. There's something to be said for introspection at various times and for specific purposes, but when introspection becomes a way of life, we'll end up feeling smothered beyond our abilities to cope. God made us to have an outward focus. There's freedom in serving others, which is one reason Scripture tells us to bear each other's burdens rather than everyone simply bearing his or her own.[15] An inward focus is its own kind of prison. Looking upward and outward sets us free.

God

I read a book years ago by Edward T. Welch titled *When People Are Big and God Is Small: Overcoming Peer Pressure,*

Codependency, and the Fear of Man.[16] I don't remember all the details of the book, but the title alone is a profound message. It points to a human tendency to magnify the things that threaten, endanger, or disturb us and to minimize God. We put a magnifying glass on our problems, turning molehills into mountains—an absurd tendency when we consider that the incomprehensibly majestic and glorious King of the universe has pledged his support for us. As Oswald Chambers once wrote, "when you fear God, you fear nothing else, whereas if you do not fear God, you fear everything else."[17] Getting a glimpse of who he is changes everything.

We've talked quite a bit about the damage done by a perception of God as a *hard* master, but it's just as damaging to see him as a *small* master. As people who are often swallowed up by our fears, we need our hearts to come to grips with the fact that he is infinitely bigger and stronger than anything we could possibly be afraid of. When John saw the glorified Jesus at the beginning of his revelation, he collapsed at his feet as though he had died.[18] The vision was that traumatic. But it's interesting that John doesn't really tremble at any of the horrific sights he sees in the rest of the book. He has already seen Jesus. Wars, plagues, a horned beast, and a bloodthirsty harlot don't seem to faze him.

It's absolutely critical to see God for who he is—and conversely, to see the threats to our security and the problems we have for what they are. He is big; they are small. The more we become aware of his majesty, the less we stress about the molehills in our lives. The theme of the next chapter will build on this truth, so I won't expand on it much here. But if any aspect of our perspectives has the power to radically change our lives and to help us live unburdened, this is it. The more we fear God, the less we fear anything else.

Just as concentrating on your sin only makes it harder to overcome, so targeting your fears and worries makes them worse. Whatever you focus on grows larger in your own mind. If you want to overcome the weight of your problems, you'll need to stop concentrating on them. You have to replace your thoughts about them with your thoughts about the power and faithfulness of God. Then you'll notice your burdens shrinking.

> **Whatever you focus on grows larger in your own mind.**

A New Perspective

It's one thing to recognize a skewed perspective and another to fix it. Recognizing it is a huge part of the process, but what can we do when we realize we've been seeing life, ourselves, or God the wrong way? I believe there are three practical steps we can take toward correcting a misguided view.

First, we need to become extremely observant of how often and in which situations that wrong perspective shows up. When we notice the ways it manifests itself, we can deal with it. When we don't notice that we're looking through the wrong lens, we think we're seeing things correctly. We have to become aware of the symptoms of a wrong perspective—heavy burdens, worries, pride, stress, anxiety, defensiveness, mistrust, etc.—and then trace those symptoms back to their sources.

That involves asking ourselves lots of questions. Why am I thinking this way? What am I afraid of? At what point do I think God isn't going to come through for me? How would I view this situation if I had the right perspective of time? the right values? a positive outlook? the right view of myself? the right view of God? Eventually, some false perspective will reveal itself.

When it does, the next step is to focus on the proper alternative. (Notice that we become *aware* of the false view but *focus* on the right one.) We've uncovered the distorted perspective, so what is the right one? How does the biblical perspective on time, values, outlook, self, and God correspond to our perspectives on these things? Once we identify that, we can tell ourselves the truth. "I'm making a big deal out of nothing." "God is bigger than this problem." "I'm not nearly as pitiful as I thought I was." "God has promised blessing, not frustration." "This isn't an eternal issue, it's a temporary one." "Things will get better." It helps to say these things out loud—as specifically and emphatically as possible. The power of the spoken word, as we've discussed, is greater than we think. Our minds and hearts listen to our own voices. The more we hear the truth from our own mouths, the more readily we accept it.

Third, choose to operate in the opposite spirit. For

example, whenever my pastor feels financial pressure, he adds an occasional dollar or two to a server's tip or gives an extra donation to a ministry or helps somebody in need. It doesn't take a lot, but "sometimes you have to remind your money that you don't serve it, it serves you," he says. He isn't being wasteful or presumptuous about God's provision; he's flowing in the opposite direction from a false perspective trying to bully him.

We can do that in a lot of ways:

- When we're too inwardly focused, we can turn our attention to the needs of others. Even one or two intentional words or actions a day can be enough to get us out of ourselves and focused outward.
- When our problems are big and God seems small, we can wake up in the morning with a different prayer. Instead of asking, "Lord, what will you do for me today to deal with these things?" we can pray, "Lord, what can I sacrifice for you today? How can I serve you? Show me at least one way." It's amazing how a couple of actions contrary to a false perspective can break that perspective's power.
- If we find ourselves focusing too much on what we lack, we can come up with a list of at least ten things we're thankful for. Our family has done this around the dinner table sometimes when we've detected a "culture of complaining" in the household. Every person has to identify at least one good thing

that happened that day and thank God for it. The glass-half-empty syndrome can't survive in that environment for long.

- When you're frustrated with your own sinfulness, grab a piece of paper and write down several scriptural statements about who you are in Christ. Read the statements to yourself five times a day—out loud while looking in a mirror—for a week. Ignore the sins you've committed. Seriously. When you ask for forgiveness, that's exactly what you're asking God to do. If you want to have his thoughts, you'll need to do the same. Overlook your trespasses and celebrate your gifts and calling. Your gifts and calling will seem to grow, and your trespasses will be stripped of their power.

That's a small sampling of the ways you can act in a contrary spirit to the false perspectives you have. You don't correct your vision simply by taking off the wrong lens prescription. You correct it by putting on the right prescription. That's what these steps do. Identify the distorted perspective wherever it shows up, tell yourself the truth that contradicts it, and then behave in an opposite spirit. Your entire outlook—your entire life—will begin to change. As Jesus promised, you will know the truth—including the right perspectives—and the truth will set you free.

CHAPTER 8

PRAISE

I HAD BEEN weighed down by a huge prayer request for a very long time. I was convinced God had promised the answer I was asking for, but the answer lingered. And lingered. And lingered some more. Anyone who has waited on God to fulfill a promise can understand the pain of waiting—and the questions that come with it. Did I hear him wrong? Have I been presumptuous? Am I believing him for something he never promised? Have I missed his answer somehow? Did I get disqualified by sinning or losing faith? How long, Lord? And on and on.

I went to a worship service one evening under the crushing weight of this prayer burden, all the questions that came with it, and the intense and frustrating longing for it to be fulfilled. And I was hardly in the mood to worship. I was even mentally venting my anger at God's ways, letting him know how rude I thought he had been to make Abraham wait twenty-five years, how he'd better not do that with me, and so on. But as the music started, I strongly sensed an instruction to worship as though God had already answered my longing. "Faith believes in spite of appearances, right?" said the voice in my mind. "It's the *assurance* of things hoped for and the *evidence* of things not seen, right? So worship as though you already have complete assurance—as though you already have the answer in hand."

I tried to imagine what that would be like, that feeling of God having just put me on the far side of the Red Sea and crushed my enemies, or of holding a promised son after twenty-five years of waiting. I envisioned the day my deep desire would be fulfilled—according to the sacred promise of a God who does not tease his children with false assurances. And the gratitude I would feel—the gratitude I *did* feel in that mental picture—was enough to send my heart soaring in the highest worship I could ever express.

So that became the heart behind my worship that night. I worshiped "as though." The music went on for at least an hour—that's typical for a worship service at my church—and I poured out my gratitude and praise for God's future gift the entire time. By the end of worship, I felt free. I had come into the building as heavy and discouraged as I had ever felt, and I left as light as a feather.

Our worship is a vital key in the quest for the unburdened life. There's something about praise and gratitude that lifts us up above our surroundings and transcends other aspects of our lives—and that brings God down, so to speak, into our circumstances. In many ways, worship is where heaven and earth meet. And the things of earth—the concerns and worries and fears that burden us—can hardly survive the encounter.

We get a graphic picture of this in the Philippian incident we looked at in chapter 6. Paul and Silas had been beaten harshly, Roman style, with thick rods that could easily break bones and damage tissue.

> **There's something about praise and gratitude that lifts us up above our surroundings and that brings God down into our circumstances.**

Their ankles were locked in painfully angled stocks, and they were left in a dark, rock-hard cell. Their ministry in Philippi was up in the air. Would they be able to remain in the city when they were freed? Would the mob that called for their imprisonment take "justice" into their own hands when they were let go? Would they even be let go at all?

Think about what it would take for you to be able to worship God in those circumstances, with everything crashing in around you. Extreme hardship does not elicit praise from the hearts of most people. The opportunities were virtually limitless for Paul and Silas to get discouraged, question God, call for legal advice, defend their rights, leave the ministry, wonder if they really were heretics like some people were saying, nurse their wounds, curse their enemies, wallow in pain, fear for their lives, and more. They could have chosen any of those options, and we would sympathize. They would be natural, understandable reactions. But if Paul and Silas had such moments, we aren't told about them. All we're told is that they "were praying and singing hymns to God, and the other prisoners were listening."[1] They were worshiping against all natural reasoning, against all expectations, and against all visible circumstances.

You're familiar with the rest of the story. God intervened with an earthquake, chains fell off, prison doors opened, and Paul prevented a distraught jailer from committing suicide in order to escape worse judgment at the hands of Roman authorities. The result was a saved household, complete vindication, and an encouraging testimony of the power of God. The incident set the stage for what would years later become the New Testament's most joyful letter.

Though many of us will never experience the kind of drama that led up to this event or that ended it, we can carry that attitude with us through any circumstance. In fact, that may be one of God's purposes in this story; if two of his servants could worship him enthusiastically in such a painful, uncomfortable crisis, we can worship him anywhere at any time. The Philippian event leaves us no room to say, "Well, it's easy to praise God when things are going well, but you don't know how difficult life has been for me." You'd be hard-pressed to think up a more grueling and distressing lifestyle than that of Paul and his companions, so their praises are a challenge to all of us. So are those of other people who praised God in terrible times. I've read of Chinese Christian leaders praising God before and after being tortured for their faith, of Sudanese children worshiping God in spite of having to watch family members be killed, of "heretics" singing hymns while being burned at the stake, and more. In light of such testimonies, is there ever an occasion in which we can legitimately assume that worshiping God is too difficult?

Gratitude

I've heard it said that thankful people are never depressed, and depressed people are never thankful. That may seem at first like a superficial judgment—and a harshly unsympathetic one too—but I've had a hard time finding an exception to the rule. As someone who has been depressed on more than one occasion, I can be sensitive to the nature of the condition. I do realize that it has various causes and can't be reduced to a simple matter of whether the depressed person is giving thanks or not. But I can also testify that an attitude of worship and gratitude—no matter how unnatural it is at first, no matter how much it goes against the grain and seems like an uphill climb—eventually has a transforming effect. It's like blowing helium into the things that weigh you down.

This was one of the secrets of a seventeenth-century monk named Nicholas Herman who spent most of his life in a small monastery in Paris. Herman never held a high position, spending most of his time serving in the kitchen, running errands, and repairing sandals. But he was so well known for his sense of peace and joy that many people, including those of much higher rank, came to him for spiritual advice. He would tell them simply to give thanks, to praise and adore God, and to carry on a continual conversation with him—all aspects of what he considered "the practice of the presence of God." His conversations and letters were later compiled in a book by that title. We know him today by the name he adopted as a monk: Brother Lawrence.

Lawrence's life was simple, but it wasn't easy. He had fought for a time in the Thirty Years' War and entered monastic life knowing he would always serve in a low position. His work was always as mundane as scrubbing pots and fixing shoes, contemptible tasks in the eyes of the world. And he did struggle for a time with a lack of satisfaction in his work. It wasn't naturally fulfilling. His only solution—the one that came to characterize his life and distinguish him from all his peers—was to place himself continually as a grateful worshiper before God, regardless of the tasks his hands were performing. He gave thanks for whatever God gave him to do. This is what gave him his deep joy and fulfillment in life.

Worship and gratitude are closely tied to that magnificent obsession we looked at earlier—the single-minded, wholehearted focus on God and his Kingdom that we pick up after we've let go of everything else. When we're centered on God, we no longer obsess about our work, family, lifestyle, ambitions, finances, or image. We obsess about his name and let him take care of the rest. Worship is the overflow of the heart that has taken that stance. It's the proof in the pudding, so to speak—the evidence that we really are more concerned with his glory than with our own interests. It's a declaration that we have a higher purpose than ourselves.

A funny thing happens when we place a higher priority on God's praises than on our own burdens. He takes up our interests as his own. He may reshape them and reprioritize them, but he begins to invest his resources in them. I believe this is what the well-known promise of Psalm 37:4 is getting at: "Take delight in the LORD, and he will give you your heart's desires." It's also the dynamic involved in Jesus' promise about prayer: "If you remain in me and my words remain in you, you may ask for anything you want, and it will be granted!"[2] God seems to become more zealous about our desires when we've abandoned ourselves to his.

We can see this in human relationships too. A loving parent will seek a child's welfare regardless of the attitudes of the child. When a child is self-absorbed, however, the parent is more focused on working on the child's attitude than on fulfilling the child's desires. But if a child is selfless, generous, loving, and genuinely concerned for the welfare of others, it's a joy for the parent to try to satisfy the child's heart. Parents *look* for ways to lavish gifts on children like that. That doesn't mean the parent loves one child more than the other; it simply means that the parent is free to focus on fulfilling the child's heart rather than correcting it.

God's love may not vary between his children, but his

willingness to defend and satisfy their desires certainly does. When we cling tightly to our own worries and concerns, he lets us. When we let go of them and cling to him, he doesn't dismiss those things we were hanging on to. He cares for them—at least the heart behind them, if not all the specifics of them—and takes them upon himself. When we choose his agenda, he takes a special interest in ours.

> **When we choose his agenda, God takes a special interest in ours.**

Grateful worship plays two parts in this process. The more obvious part is the role of worship as an expression of our focus on God. When he and his Kingdom are our obsession, gratitude will inevitably flow out of our hearts and mouths. But worship is also a powerful catalyst for getting us out of ourselves and into that single obsession to begin with. It's not only the outcome of a Godward focus; it's a means to it. As an outcome, it flows from us naturally. As a means, it's an act of the will—a choice we make regardless of how we feel. But when we are able to make that choice and praise God regardless of our moods, the burdens we carry, and the circumstances we're struggling through, our attitudes begin to change. Our spirits seem to step into the picture our praises have drawn.

The Power of Words

The Bible is very clear that words have power. In Scripture, they are concrete entities, which is why spoken blessings couldn't just be "taken back" and why Balaam wasn't allowed to utter a curse against Israel.[3] Words are treated as substance in Scripture—*tangible* substance. Even a cursory reading of a few key passages on the power of words is impressive:

Then God said . . . and it was.[4]

The tongue can bring death or life.[5]

If we could control our tongues, we would be perfect and could also control ourselves in every other way. . . . The tongue is a small thing that makes grand speeches. But a tiny spark can set a great forest on fire. And the tongue is a flame of fire. It is a whole world of wickedness, corrupting your entire body. It can set your whole life on fire, for it is set on fire by hell itself. People can tame all kinds of animals, birds, reptiles, and fish, but no one can tame the tongue. It is restless and evil, full of deadly poison. Sometimes it praises our Lord and Father, and sometimes it curses those who have been made in the image of God. And so blessing and cursing come pouring out of the same mouth.[6]

Do not let any unwholesome talk come out of your mouths, but only what is helpful for building others up according to their needs, that it may benefit those who listen.[7]

*I tell you this, you must give an account on judgment day
for every idle word you speak.*[8]

Studies in psychology and sociology affirm that words
are powerful, though we hardly need scientific research to
tell us that. We know from history and personal experience
that words can incite riots, inspire movements, start wars,
build esteem, inflict wounds, sway opinions, prove guilt or
innocence, and more. Sticks and stones may break our bones,
but words can do much worse than that. We've felt both the
pain of negative words and the pleasure of positive ones. We
know how one comment can sink us into despair or cause
us to soar. Words—the expression of human thoughts—can
change the course of a day and even a life.

That's why what we say to ourselves is critically important. That's true for our internal thought processes, but even
more so for the words that come out of our mouths. Our self-
talk, as psychological studies and common sense can affirm,
has tremendous power over how we see life and how we react
to the people around us and the situations we find ourselves
in. A pattern of negative self-talk sends us on a downward
spiral into discouragement, depression, fear, and doubt; and
a pattern of positive self-talk builds us up and empowers us
to trust, believe, be courageous and confident, and experience joy and peace.

I've seen this at work in my life repeatedly. For example,
I've let an unexpected car repair start me on a path of spec-
ulating about how that month's bills might not get paid,

which in turn makes me second-guess my ability to manage money in general, and maybe I'm not even in the right job if the budget is always this tight, and what if the economy doesn't improve and, in the midst of a recession, I get laid off? Before long, my mind is spinning with negative thoughts and even accusations at God for letting me get into the horrible predicament I'm in, even though most of the horrible predicament is still in my mind and hasn't happened yet. I've also let a simple disagreement with someone fuel endless speculation about that person's motives, the possibility that he or she might be pulling strings behind the scenes and manipulating situations that affect me, giving other people a false impression about me or someone I love, and planning to undermine my goals or wishes by asserting his or her own agenda instead. Before you call that paranoid, think about ways you may have done the same sort of thing. We human beings have an enormous capacity to escalate situations in our own minds.

Unless you're one of the few naturally laid-back people in this world who rarely worry, you've probably noticed that 90 percent of the things you worry about never happen. And you've also probably noticed that *all* of the things you worry about are fueled by negative self-talk. So is most of the shame and guilt you feel—a lot of that comes from the wounds of childhood and thought patterns that were established long ago. And so are most of the doubts you have about whether God is going to come through for you. You can talk yourself out of just about anything.

There's no need to belabor this point because you know what it's like for thoughts to swirl around in your brain when you'd rather be sleeping or enjoying some downtime. Everyone does. And you know how much more powerful those churning thoughts become when they start to infect your speech and you voice them out loud. Your worst fears can seem to become more and more like concrete reality the more you talk about them. Only reversing the trend with positive self-talk and affirming speech can break the power of the lies we think and breathe.

That's where worship comes in. We recognize our negative thought and speech patterns about as well as fish recognize water. In other words, not at all. They are the environment we swim in. Consciously choosing to praise God in spite of our current "environment" is a forceful way to break out of it. Nothing does a better job of lifting us out of the conditions that burden us and crush us. Nothing stops the downward spiral more effectively. Nothing jolts us out of the things we're mired in better than a reminder that we are above them—and more important, that we are integrally connected with the all-powerful being who is never constrained or crushed by anything. When we worship, God gets dramatically bigger in our own eyes and the rest of our issues get dramatically smaller. Choosing to praise him

Consciously choosing to praise God in spite of our current "environment" is a forceful way to break out of it.

is more liberating than any medication on the market or any therapeutic technique in the world. It's a burden breaker.

Army-officer-turned-pastor Merlin Carothers wrote several best-selling books on this topic years ago, the best known of which are *Prison to Praise* and *Power in Praise*. The first was an autobiographical account of how praise transformed him from an angry, unmotivated, fearful young rebel into a confident and joyful minister. After reading *Prison to Praise*, numerous people wrote Carothers to tell him how the book had changed their lives, many of them explaining in great detail how God had worked in their circumstances in response to their praise. The second book expanded on the same theme; it included many of those testimonies about the first book and gave further examples of the transforming power of praise from Carothers's own ministry experiences.[9] Though the principle comes across as simplistic to many people—and it's true that the books never attempt to fully explore all the relevant theological issues—the testimonies are undeniable. After all, God didn't craft his Kingdom so that only the intellectual elite could grab hold of it. He made it highly accessible. The lives of real people *have* changed, both inwardly and outwardly, when they choose to praise God in every circumstance. God seems to step into our circumstances in dramatic ways when we focus our worship on him.

I've tried this principle of praising God in all situations, no matter how negative they seem, and I've been profoundly affected by the results. For much of my life, I've naturally tended toward pessimism, and I have to fight discouragement almost as vigorously as if it's a sin. So even though worship should be the easiest thing in the world for a person filled with God's Spirit, it's a huge effort sometimes. But God seems to honor my efforts to fight through pessimistic mental habits and emotional patterns. I can't really explain how that works. All I know is that good things happen when I'm thankful and praising God.

I know many people—myself included—sometimes raise two objections to the idea of thanking God in all circumstances. One is that "yes, but" tendency we talked about earlier. It usually sounds something like, "Yes, I know that God is always worthy of worship, but if I'm trying to praise him even when I don't feel like it, then isn't that being fake?" And it's true that it feels really hypocritical to praise God when your heart isn't in it. But if God is always worthy of praise, then praising him is always the right thing to do. Worshiping when you don't feel like it is correcting a huge wrong. We don't have to tell God we feel wonderful about him when we don't—that *would* be fake—but we can tell him we know he's wonderful even though we aren't feeling the love. There's nothing hypocritical about that. It's truth.

The other objection is that worshiping God when we feel burdened and overwhelmed, knowing that "good things" happen when we worship him, feels manipulative. If my experience has been that God responds positively to my praise by bursting into my circumstances or at least improving my mood, then the temptation is to start praising him in order to get something from him. That's a genuine temptation and a habit we don't want to develop. But what's the alternative? To refuse to worship him simply because we know he'll probably respond favorably? That doesn't make any sense either. There has to be an honest, in-between response.

The balance that seems to make the most sense to me is to say something like, "Lord, I know that worshiping you makes your presence more manifest in my life, and I honestly do want the benefits you bring. But deep down, I also want you. I can't really separate you from your benefits, and I'm doing my best not to manipulate you. But I also know that worship puts our relationship in its proper place. Give me the grace to worship you as though your blessings aren't going to flow back to me in response—and the gratitude that comes from knowing they will."

God is fine with an honest prayer like that. He understands our frailties. If he refused to relate to us whenever we had mixed motives, he would never relate to us. He knows we come to him wanting not only him but also what he gives. In fact, he often encourages us to seek his blessings. "Let all that I am praise the LORD; may I never forget the good things he does for me,"[10] and the psalm continues with an unapologetic list of God's blessings. We don't want to be selfishly manipulative, but both he and we know we aren't so completely God-centered that we come to him unaware of the ways we benefit from him. He gives us a lot of freedom to enjoy his gifts and even seek them. He *likes* us to worship him for his blessings and to pursue them. It's okay to know the good results of our praise.

One of those good results is how he comes to the defense of those who love him. In the midst of brutal circumstances in which it seems like all of life is conspiring against me, I've thanked him that his purposes can't be thwarted, that everything the enemy throws into a situation will actually serve to advance it somehow, and that he puts his people in no-lose positions. When a believer is trusting, thanking, and praising God regardless of what he or she is going through, losing is impossible. Anything the world or the enemy tries to do to oppose someone who trusts God is like trying to stamp out a grease fire. The fire only spreads.

We see this clearly in the book of Acts. The Christian movement began to spread, and it was attacked from numerous angles. Political and religious authorities persecuted Christian leaders, sin tried to creep its way into the fellowship, disagreements broke out among leaders, and factions developed among groups of believers. But persecution served to strengthen the faith of Christians and scatter them into the world to spread the truth. The sin of Ananias and Sapphira demonstrated God's zeal for the purity of his church and inspired awe among its members and observers.[11] Disagreements among leaders gave them the opportunity to sort out key doctrines and beliefs that would

> **Anything the world or the enemy tries to do to oppose someone who trusts God is like trying to stamp out a grease fire. The fire only spreads.**

form our Scripture and inform the church for millennia to come. And factions within churches eventually did more to prove the unified diversity of the body of Christ than to fracture it. The vibrant lives of worship, praise, and gratitude of people like Peter and John before the Sanhedrin (Acts 4) or Paul and Silas in Philippi (Acts 16) always prompted God's defense and resulted in more awe and praise.

That doesn't mean God won't allow strategic sacrifices like those of Stephen and James. Both were martyred during the early years of the church, and it wasn't because they didn't know how to praise God in difficult times. Even so, God defended his mission zealously, and if we believe in his sovereignty at all, we have to conclude that not a single faithful believer was harmed outside of his purposes. That may be of little comfort to someone burdened about all the bad things that can happen, but somehow Peter, who knew all about the martyrdom of Stephen and James, could still sleep the night before he thought he might be executed. He could be at peace because the very worst that can happen to a believer in Jesus who trusts God is death and instant fellowship with Jesus at God's right hand—where, by the way, we are assured of "pleasures forevermore."[12] That won't calm the hearts of people who haven't let go of their own agendas, but it's enormously reassuring to those who have. The ultimate "disaster" for a Christian is the ultimate gift. If we really do trust God with all our burdens, we have nothing to worry about.

That frees us up to be worshipful in any situation, no matter how threatening it appears. No weapon raised against us can succeed.[13] The only real threat we face is not whether our circumstances will work out but whether we can maintain our faith, gratitude, and worship in the process. Jesus promised that all things are possible for those who believe. So if we're preoccupied with all the potential problems in our lives, thinking that the real battle is successfully controlling the outcomes, we're missing the truth. The real battle is over our attitudes and perspectives. If we can maintain faith and continue to acknowledge who God is, the eventual outcomes will be greater than we imagined. There might be some bumps along the way, but God works all things out in the end for those whose grateful worship stays intact. Even Job, crushed under more terrible weights than most of us will ever know, maintained his worship and was doubly blessed in the end. God promises to do more than we can even ask or imagine—a promise that, not coincidentally, is the culmination of a passage in which Paul is overflowing with praise.[14] That kind of attitude is invincible, and God's good purposes in the life of someone with that attitude are impossible to thwart.

This is why joy, rejoicing, and celebration are supposed to be such integral parts of our relationship with God. We think circumstances are the battlefield, and then joy usually follows when circumstances work out. But it's really the other way around. Worship and joy are the battlefield, and then circumstances usually shift when the attitudes of the heart work out. The circumstances may not change immediately or dramatically—though they very often do, in miraculous and surprising ways—but God always responds to a right heart by stepping into those things the heart has been concerned about. One way or another, he intervenes on behalf of those who look to him in praise and gratitude. He has emphatically promised to do so throughout Scripture, and he always keeps his promises.

That explains why Paul was able to command the Philippians to rejoice. You can't command a feeling, but you can command a choice, and he wanted the Philippians to choose the attitudes of the Kingdom. Joy is the climate of heaven, and that's where we want our hearts to live. So Paul instructed joy to people whose circumstances were difficult, whose brain chemistry may have been predisposed to depression, whose careers may have been downwardly mobile, and who were worried about things like persecution and dissension. There were no exceptions to this command, no caveats, no extenuating circumstances that excused certain people from following it. The same apostle who sang hymns while in prison and in pain had ample authority to tell the Philippians to get over their anxiety and praise God. Why? Because that's the key, and that's where the battle takes place.

Lessons from the Field Manual

I've referred earlier to the Psalms as a field manual in the unburdened life. Quite a few of them begin with the writer, often David, in some sort of deep distress. But almost invariably, the attitude changes by the end of the psalm. One of the reasons for the emotional shift is the choices the psalmist makes. You'll notice declarations of "I will" throughout these prayers and songs. "I *will* praise you," "I *will* sing a new song to you," "I *will* bless the Lord," "I *will* worship at your temple," "I *will* thank the Lord," and on and on. That's because in hard times, worship is a choice.

I believe these declarations of the will are great examples of the psalmist changing his self-talk from negative, faithless, fearful statements to positive, faith-filled, trusting statements.

> In hard times, worship is a choice.

We've seen that in Psalm 103, for instance, in which David begins by speaking to himself and making deliberate choices about his attitude: "Praise the LORD, *I tell myself*, with my whole heart, I *will* praise his holy name. Praise the LORD, *I tell myself*, and never forget the good things he does for me."[15] And then he goes on and reminds himself of exactly what the Lord does for him: he forgives sins, heals diseases, saves from death, renews youth, fills life with good things, and delivers justice.

He begins Psalm 9 in a similar way: "I *will* praise you, LORD, with all my heart; I *will* tell of all the marvelous things you have done. I *will* be filled with joy because of you. I *will* sing praises to your name, O Most High."[16] And then, significantly, he continues with declarations of how his enemies are being turned away and how God is judging rightly from his throne. And again in Psalm 34: "I *will* praise the LORD at all times. I *will* constantly speak his praises. I *will* boast only in the LORD; let all who are helpless take heart. Come, let us tell of the LORD's greatness; let us exalt his name together."[17] And the next verse is a statement about how God has delivered him from his fears.

Psalm 91 is one of the most popular passages in the Psalter, primarily because of its antiworry, burden-busting words of assurance. Again, it begins with a choice and a declaration to the self: "I will say of the LORD, 'He is my refuge and my fortress, my God, in whom I trust.'"[18] And Psalm 42 is essentially a conversation between David and his own soul. He's talking to himself, instructing himself to snap out of discouragement and praise God:

> *Why are you downcast, O my soul? Why so disturbed within me? Put your hope in God, for I will yet praise him. . . . I say to God my Rock, "Why have you forgotten me? Why must I go about mourning, oppressed by the enemy?" My bones suffer mortal agony as my foes taunt me, saying to me all day long, "Where is your God?" Why are you downcast, O my soul? Why so disturbed within me? Put your hope in God, for I will yet praise him, my Savior and my God.*[19]

And in the same spirit that enabled Peter to rest in prison, David knew how to make a profound choice to go to sleep: "In peace I will lie down and sleep, for you alone, O LORD, will keep me safe."[20] Again and again in these models of prayer and praise, the people of God instruct their own hearts, often with spoken words, about which attitude to adopt.

The words of the Psalms are not random statements of praise. They are targeted at situations and spoken in specific crises. These affirmations were written for the psalmists themselves, not just for readers thousands of years later. These model prayers show us how to interrupt the fearful, doubting, burdensome thoughts swirling around in our heads with statements of truth. No matter how heavy you feel when you begin reading one of these psalms, you feel lighter by the end of it if you've read it thoughtfully and embraced what it says. These are extremely valuable case studies in the power of worship to break us out of our distress and deliver us from the heavy loads of life.

Gratefully worshiping God in any circumstance is a choice. It may be a choice that goes against deeply ingrained habits and thought patterns, but it's still a real, viable option. It may be a choice that takes persistence and time to implement, but it's still powerful and effective. It may be a choice that we think is superficial, hypocritical, or much too simplistic, but we should expect such false accusations, even coming from within our own hearts and minds. We have an enemy who is zealously and violently opposed to true worship and to people who connect with God and overcome the world.

On the other side of this choice, when we are able to make it decisively and stick with it, is freedom. When the magnificent obsession plays its way out through our mouths and our lifestyles, burdens lose their power.

CHAPTER 9

PRESENCE

THE SEA WAS unpredictable. Usually it was calm, but sudden storms were not uncommon. And normally it yielded a good catch, but a whole night of empty nets wasn't a huge surprise. Regardless, it was always a symbol of the untamed chaos of Genesis 1:2—the tumultuous, mysterious deep.

Peter had spent much of his life on this sea. It was where he earned his livelihood—and where he would worry about his livelihood if earnings were hard to come by. It was where he spent long, dark nights trying to harvest a catch before daybreak or strong winds interfered. To any fisherman of his time, it was a necessary means of survival, the impersonal arbiter between success and failure and between rest and toil.

If Peter was ever going to learn any lessons on life, labor, and looking to God for help, the sea would be the best possible classroom.

Jesus seemed to know that; he had a way of revealing truth in the midst of storms and fishing expeditions. One of the earliest lessons he taught Peter came after one of those long, dark nights with nothing but empty nets. While several fishermen were cleaning up after their night of futility, Jesus borrowed Peter's boat to use as a speaking platform and then, after his message, urged these professional fishermen to launch back out into the deep at the wrong time of day for fishing. The result was astonishing. The catch was so large that the nets began to break. Jesus' presence—his inside information, his instructions, his revealed purposes—made all the difference.

About three years later, this harvest-inducing presence was one way Jesus revealed his identity to his friends from a distance after the Resurrection. Peter and several other disciples had gone fishing but had caught nothing—again. At daybreak, a man on the shore shouted to them, asking whether they had any fish. No, they had to admit.

> The ultimate key to the unburdened life is having the life of the unburdened one within us.

Then the distant figure told them to fish from the other side of the boat, and for some reason they gave it a try. Again, the enormity of the catch practically broke the net. The disciples could hardly pull it in. They knew instantly that the figure on the shore was Jesus. His presence had once again made a difference.

The same presence is available to us—and can make just as dramatic a difference in our lives. Everything we've discussed to this point can be helpful, but the only real, lasting change comes from cultivating the presence of Jesus. If we want our burdens to be light, we need the Burden Bearer to be with us. In order to have that *shalom* we so desperately seek, we need the Prince of Shalom to bring it. Apart from him, all we have is a set of techniques to reduce our stress and change our perspectives. The techniques can be very effective, but they aren't supernatural without his presence. The ultimate key to the unburdened life is having the life of the unburdened one within us.

The Life Within

It was my turn to lead our weekly staff prayer time, which usually includes a devotional thought or two before we start taking prayer requests. I decided this time to add a little twist to the conversation. Instead of printing out some Bible verses we already have a handle on, I made a short list of "Verses We Don't Believe." The initial reaction to the title was, as I had hoped, a good chuckle among the few of us around the table. And the conversation, as I also had hoped, stretched us a little uncomfortably.

Most Christians can probably think of several verses we

think we believe but actually don't—at least not in our gut and in a way that makes a difference in how we live. There are plenty such truths to choose from. The ones I chose on this day for our devotional time were all related to our unity with Jesus and his Spirit:

> *I have been crucified with Christ and I no longer live, but Christ lives in me.*[1]

> *I have given them the glory you gave me, so that they may be one, as we are—I in them and you in me, all being perfected into one."*[2]

> *He . . . seated us with him in the heavenly realms because we are united with Christ Jesus.*[3]

> *. . . that you may be filled to the measure of all the fullness of God.*[4]

> *It is God who works in you to will and to act according to his good purpose.*[5]

These are astounding verses if we take them at face value, but the problem is that they are so astounding we usually *don't* take them at face value. We hyperspiritualize them or project them off into the millennial Kingdom, even though they are all in present or past tense, or else we see them as theological statements of our positions in Christ without implementing these truths in any practical way. We love them and claim them and memorize them, but we rarely ever live them.

Our discomfort with these "favorite" verses really shows up when we speak of them as our reality. Imagine, for example, that the first words out of my mouth when I stood up at a podium were, "Thanks for inviting me to speak tonight. I just want to assure you that it really isn't me, it's Jesus. I have his glory, and he and I have just as close a bond as he and our Father have. I've been living and ruling throneside with him the last few years and am filled with all of God's fullness. So I suspect that my words tonight will be no ordinary event, since God has completely shaped me and is working out his thoughts and purposes through me."

I'm pretty sure my seeming arrogance would elicit a negative response and ensure that I'd never be invited to speak there again. And, in fact, I would be ashamed and embarrassed to even utter such words. But which of them, according to Scripture, aren't true of every believer? Aren't they all solidly biblical facts? Can these truths have any practical relevance for us if we're embarrassed to even admit that they are practically relevant? You see my point, I'm sure. These are verses we don't believe—at least not at face value.

No, we place an awful lot of faith in the fact of our sinful natures—we talk about it much more than we talk about having Jesus' glory within us, you know—and we spend a lot of time talking about the sin we're supposed to consider ourselves dead to. We speak of our struggles and circumstances as though they constrained us rather than speaking of our positions seated high above them. By our own misinformed testimonies, our old natures are remarkably alive for something that was crucified with Jesus. And we strain far too hard to reach a God who, according to Jesus, is meant to be as close to us as the members of the Trinity are to each other. It's very clear that our perceptions don't line up with these truths.

Why? Because for all our affirmations of the priority of God's Word over our own experiences, we still interpret his Word through our experiences. We look at these astounding truths, measure them against our own lives, and decide that the words must mean something other than what they say.

A lot of theology is done this way, and it's unavoidable to a degree. Sometimes our experiences really do shed light on what Scripture means to say. But when we get in the habit of trying to bring the lofty truths of Scripture down to our levels of experience, rather than trying to bring our levels of experience up to the lofty truths of Scripture, we miss out on a lot. We make assumptions we shouldn't make and settle for less than what God intended.

My point is that we read some unimaginably glorious statements in the Bible assuring us that we are empowered by the spiritual resources of God himself, and we hardly know what to do with them. They become nothing more than statements—theological truths that have little impact on how we handle the events of a particular day. We have heaven's resources at our disposal, and little knowledge of how to access them. The result is that we believe in God's supernatural provision without actually experiencing it.

So how exactly does this relate to the unburdened life? Ultimately, our abilities to live in freedom depend on being empowered by another life within us. Our flesh is crushed by its burdens, but the Spirit can't be. If we see the amazing facts of our unity with Christ and the indwelling of his Spirit as theoretical principles, we'll inevitably be burdened. We'll have no choice, unless we go with one of those counterfeit options we discussed in chapter 1, like abdicating responsibility or detaching spiritually. If we actually experience the facts of our unity with Christ and the indwelling of his Spirit, then we can live in freedom.

Notice that the issue isn't what we believe, at least not in the sense of our mental agreements with truth. The issue is what we apply—how we actually live. All Bible-believing Christians would agree with the verses printed above. We even memorize them and quote them. The problem is that where the rubber meets the road—i.e., when we're in the middle of a crisis or operating out of past wounds or juggling overwhelming burdens—we don't actually function from these truths. We don't stop and tell ourselves, *Wait a minute—the power of God himself will deal with this issue. I have no need to worry about it.* It's one thing to *say* that Jesus is living in us, and quite another to really let him. A lot of us say he is. Few of us give him the freedom in real life to be himself within us.

> It's one thing to *say* that Jesus is living in us, and quite another to really let him.

There's a neighborhood in Atlanta that I have trouble navigating. This isn't unusual; most of Atlanta isn't laid out on a grid, and with all the trees and hills limiting your view and forcing roads to wind around, it's easy to lose your bearings. I have a pretty good sense of direction, so I always think I can cut through this particular neighborhood and end up on the street I'm trying to get to. But every time I've tried cutting from one major street to the one on the other side of the neighborhood, I've ended up completely turned around. I go through four-way stops and perpendicular stops, I've tried turning right here and left there, and vice versa, and inevitably when I finally see the bustling traffic of a major road and think I've finally made it through, I find out that the major road I'm seeing is the same one I turned off of in the first place. I've wound around without making any real progress.

One day, I finally made it through that neighborhood. Well, I say I made it . . . but I really got through because I had someone in the car with me who knew the way. When I would get to an intersection, my fellow traveler would tell me which way to go. This was a genuine exercise in trust because some of the turns he directed me on were so counterintuitive that I seriously doubted he knew what he was talking about. I had to reject my own wisdom and depend on his. But apparently he did know what he was talking about because I finally found the route I had always searched for. When I switched off my dependence on my own resources and reasoning and instead relied on my guide, I got to my destination.

In some respects, that's the dynamic involved in letting go of burdens. You have to actually abandon your own understanding and lean on God's.[6] That requires a lot of trust because there are moments when you feel like you're being led in exactly the wrong way. When you relinquish control, circumstances may initially get worse and cause you to question your guide. You'll be seriously tempted to take the controls back and navigate your own way. It may feel irresponsible not to worry and feel the weight of your burdens because if the one you've given them to isn't really carrying them—and it may seem as if he isn't—then no one is. You'll have to trust that you haven't deserted your responsibilities by letting them go. But if you can continue in trust and let him navigate your way and carry your load, the result will be worth it.

This is one small glimpse of the exchanged life, which is really as comprehensive as we're willing to let it be. It not only applies to the wisdom and direction God will give us if we lean on his mind instead of our own, it also applies to the strength by which we live. This is the exchange Hudson Taylor experienced after years of fruitfulness in his storied ministry. It's hard to imagine someone with such zeal and effectiveness for God needing a new revelation of truth, but Taylor described his discovery of "the exchanged life" in terms of being "a new man." Mr. Judd, a colleague in China, described the change:

He was a joyous man now, a bright happy Christian. He had been a toiling, burdened one before, with latterly not much rest of soul. It was resting in Jesus now, and letting Him do the work—which makes all the difference. Whenever he spoke in meetings after that, a new power seemed to flow from him, and in the practical things of life a new peace possessed him. Troubles did not worry him as before. He cast everything on God in a new way.[7]

This is the kind of change we all want. We crave the ability to do all we have to do with freedom and rest rather than burdens and stress. Ultimately, the only way to do that is to realize the power that works within us—*and* to rely on that Spirit of power to do his work.

Make It Sink In

The fact is that my list of "verses we don't believe" all point to this exchanged life. Admittedly, this is something beyond our abilities to understand, but it's still fully within our abilities to apply. If these truths weren't applicable, they would be frivolous intrusions into sacred Scripture. God made us for a relationship with him, and he breathed his Word in order to establish and build that relationship. He is not the kind of God to give us superfluous information.

We know, of course, that these magnificent truths are not superfluous. No Christian claims that they are. We simply *act* as if they are sometimes. But plenty of people throughout history have found in these truths a power beyond themselves and an ability to rise above their circumstances and to live freely. How? By actually believing them. The exchanged life is a real possibility. These sacred realities become powerfully effective when they somehow, someway, sink into our hearts.

Only God can really reveal these things to us at a practical level, but there are some things we can do to make them more real to us. I've found it helpful to read the above verses to myself out loud repeatedly, persistently, and stubbornly, looking myself in the eyes in a mirror while I'm doing it. This isn't so much to gain the knowledge of what these verses are saying but to let the reality of Jesus' presence with me and in me sink in. As Brother Lawrence showed, the presence of God is a practice. Sometimes you have to convince yourself he's there first, but then you simply need to be aware. Having a running conversation with him helps. Picturing him sitting in a chair across the table or in the passenger seat of the car while you drive helps too. Sensing his presence and power deep within you is vital. In some ways, it's a discipline to continue knowing that he is there. But it's a discipline that eventually becomes natural.

It takes more than this, of course. We aren't just trying to convince ourselves of truth. We are invoking the name of a real Being who is passionately committed to those who love him. So what do you do when you need something from another person? You ask. The only way to find the restful, liberated life we want to live is to ask and keep asking.

I'll share some things I've said to God in this conversation, not to give you a formula to follow but to help get you started. There are thousands of variations of these words; these just happen to be the ones that ended up in my journals and my memory. You've probably prayed some of these things before, or at least something very similar. If so, I would encourage you to keep praying them and to be as bluntly honest with

God invites us to take hold of what he offers and to hang on to it boldly and tenaciously.

God as you know how to be. He loves the kind of honesty that takes him at his Word and insists that his Word must be true. He responds to the stubborn persistence of his children. He invites us to take hold of what he offers and to hang on to it boldly and tenaciously. These prayers are my way of doing that, and I trust that they will help you do that too.

- Father, you want me to live lightly. I want to live lightly. We agree on this prayer, so let it be. Amen.
- Lord, you promise to give me all I need. I don't trust you enough, I don't have the right perspectives, I don't worship you enough, I have a hard time letting go of my burdens, and I have a hard time pursuing you single-mindedly. But these are attitudes and abilities that I desperately need. As you promised, help me

through your power to trust, see, worship, let go, and seek your Kingdom above all else.

- Lord, you have promised amazing things and used some pretty extravagant language to describe our relationship with you. I don't want to miss out on *anything* you're calling me into. I don't want for a second to rely on my own strength when yours is available. And honestly, I don't want to carry these burdens anymore. I don't want to lie awake at night with worrisome thoughts swirling around in my head. The only thoughts I want keeping me up are the words you want me to hear from your mind and your heart. Only you can help me with that. So please help.

- Father, there's a lot on my plate right now. A lot of it is too hard for me to deal with. Frankly, I don't want to go through these trials at all. I do want to be responsible and complete the work you've given me to do, but I'm tired and worn down. You promised strength. You said you were giving me your Spirit. You told me I'm dead and Jesus is alive in me. If you mean those things at all—and I know you do—then deliver on your promise. I'm taking you at your word. I'm going to refuse to be weighed down by all of the things I'm facing. I'm letting them go and trusting you to pick them up. If you don't, then you and I both look bad. Especially me—I'll look really irresponsible. But I know you won't betray my trust. You promised.

- You commanded me not to worry. So I won't. Period.
- Thank you, Lord, for this crisis. You know I'm not thrilled about it, so I hope you don't see my "gratitude" as a sham. But I know how you work, and I know you'll deliver. If Israel knew what the Red Sea would eventually mean to them, they would have thanked you on the front side of it. If Lazarus knew how his illness and death would be used in your Word and for your glory, he would have embraced it wholeheartedly ahead of time. So as much as it goes against my grain, I'm thanking you for what this crisis will come to symbolize in my future: your glory, your power, your willingness to intervene in my life.
- I absolutely refuse to be anxious about this. If I perish, I perish. So be it. But for now, Lord, help me rest and be at peace.
- Lord, this is your problem, not mine. Help me take my hands off of it. You promise to be my Savior? Then save. You call yourself my Deliverer? Then deliver. You call yourself my Healer? Then heal. You call yourself my Provider? Then provide. I don't mean any of that disrespectfully. I just know that you glorify yourself by stepping into our needs. Well, I have needs, and I'm calling upon your name. The next step is yours—just as you want it to be.
- You promise to renew my strength. You promise to live inside of me and to *be* my life. I want everything that entails at whatever cost it entails. Whatever

soaring with wings like an eagle's means, whatever walking on water represents, whatever living by your Spirit implies, I want that. All of it. Teach me. Help me. Make these things a reality in my life. Amen and amen.

Conclusion

THE KING WAS buckling under the pressure. The threats mounting against him were beyond his ability to handle. Three armies had combined to surround the region with one goal in mind: wipe out this one vulnerable, in-the-way kingdom. And this wasn't just any kingdom; it was God's chosen nation. The stakes were high. God's purposes were on the line; the king's life and the lives of his entire family were on the line; and the welfare of a small but important people was on the line. The king and his people had every reason to be thoroughly overwhelmed. So he called for a nationwide fast, and leaders from all over the country came to the capital to cry out to God.

Life can't get much more stressful than that. It's a heavy burden for an entire nation to look to you for leadership and strength, and when your army is a sitting duck for three allied enemies . . . well, desperate times call for desperate measures.

That's why Jehoshaphat called for a fast, and that's why

Judah's people gathered at the Temple in Jerusalem to seek God's favor. They appealed to the facts of history: God had chosen this people for the glory of his own name, and he had brought them into this land centuries earlier—even forbidding them from attacking these very enemies on their way through the wilderness. And now these enemies had arisen to wipe out God's people. Surely he would come to their aid.

But how? Judah's army was no match for this alliance. And what if God had changed his mind about his people? Their recent history of keeping God's commandments and worshiping him alone wasn't very impressive.[1] What if he was about to teach them a lesson? What if those stories of his past miracles and rescues had been exaggerated? What if God was going to demonstrate his glory in some unexpected way, like letting Judah be defeated and then raising it up again under new leadership? What if he wanted to teach his people to be faithful even in the worst of times? This situation could play out in a multitude of ways, and only one of them—a miraculous rescue—would be satisfying. But miraculous rescues don't happen every day. This one was a long shot.

Regardless, you don't have many alternatives when three armies, each one stronger than your own, join forces and surround you. Crying out to God is about all you can do. And when God has filled your history with powerful deeds and promises, there's always hope. So Jehoshaphat dropped all pretense—no posing, no bargaining, no self-directed agenda, and no hint of self-sufficiency—and simply expressed his position: "We are powerless against this mighty army that is about to attack us. We do not know what to do, but we are looking to you for help."[2]

God answered by gripping one man named Jahaziel with his Spirit and inspiring a prophetic word. It was a message instructing the king and his people to stop worrying, to be courageous, to refuse to get discouraged, and, most surprisingly, not to even fight the battle. This battle would be God's responsibility, not theirs. He would take up this burden. They wouldn't have to carry it at all.

Jehoshaphat could have been suspicious of this prophecy. For all he knew, Jahaziel could have been struck with religious fervor and been declaring what he would like to happen. His zeal could have been wishful thinking with a spiritual twist. He was just one priest among many; how could Jehoshaphat know this word was from the Lord? Would God really want his people to stand still in a time of crisis? If this word was off base, the entire nation would soon experience disaster. Following it would require an awful lot of trust. Jehoshaphat would have to let go of his expectations and his pride—kings don't get much public affirmation when they defer leadership to God and do none of the fighting—and rest his hopes completely in God's ability to deliver.

Would God really want his people to stand still in a time of crisis?

Jehoshaphat did accept this prophecy as a word from the Lord, and he and his people bowed their faces to the ground and worshiped. The threat remained; the hostile armies were still ominously approaching. But now, after a single promise from God—or a priest who *said* he got a message from God—the appropriate response was worship. Praise. Gratitude. With a devastating threat still on the horizon.

Early the next morning, Judah's army went out into the wilderness where the alliance was advancing. Jehoshaphat tried to build the confidence of his troops, urging them to believe God, stand firm, and trust the word of a prophet. Then, after consulting other leaders, he arranged for worshipers to lead the way. God had given no instructions on how the warriors were to proceed to the battlefield. This was the king's idea. But if God had promised to fight for his people—and, in fact, had commanded his people *not* to fight but to keep their hands off the burden they had entrusted him with—then worship before battle made perfect sense.

> Instead of the warriors going out to fight, hoping their God would support them, God went out to fight as the warrior with his people supporting him.

This scene completely rearranged the expected roles of the main characters. Instead of the normal approach—the warriors going out to fight, hoping their God would support them—God went out to fight as the warrior with his people supporting him.

It's important to notice that these two possible approaches were mutually exclusive. It's impossible to trust God to fight a battle and then send out your warriors with weapons in hand to face the enemy, especially when God has said to take your positions but then stand still. Jehoshaphat must have wrestled with some tension between "going" and "standing," but he had to make a choice. The prophet had said to march out, but also to stand still. God had instructed Judah not to fight. What does "not fighting" look like when an army marches out to meet an enemy? Jehoshaphat arrived at a sensible but very creative solution. There would be marching, but on behalf of God. The worshipers would lead the way.

So Judah advanced to the singing and chanting of its praise team. They worshiped God for his holy splendor, even while hostile Ammonites, Moabites, and Meunites sharpened their swords. They shouted their gratitude to God—"Give thanks to the Lord; his faithful love endures forever!"[3]—even while surrounded by warriors who wanted to wipe them out. They cast their burdens on the Lord even while their circumstances breathed deadly threats. They refused to carry the weight of this situation.

The outcome is well known to most people familiar with the Bible. "At the very moment [Judah] began to sing and give praise,"[4] the three hostile armies turned on each other, their alliance crumbled, and their infighting tore them to shreds. When Judah's army arrived, they found only the dead bodies of a once-ominous enemy. Not only was the kingdom spared, its relative power in the region was greatly strengthened. Three of their greatest enemies were severely weakened, they gathered massive wealth by plundering the defeated enemies on the battlefield, and their reputation as God-protected people spread.

This remarkable story of 2 Chronicles 20 is an example for us. It's a graphic picture of what happens when God's people let go of an overwhelming burden and radically trust God to deal with it. We see the intense stress of a life-threatening situation, a decision to let go of human reasoning and worry and fear, a decision to adopt a Kingdom perspective, a radical trust in God that included a shift from focusing on enemies and challenges to focusing on him alone, a choice to worship and praise God regardless of how circumstances look, and a dramatic intervention by the divine hand. What was the result?

> *Then all the men returned to Jerusalem, with Jehoshaphat leading them, overjoyed that the LORD had given them victory over their enemies. They marched into Jerusalem to the music of harps, lyres, and trumpets, and they proceeded to the Temple of the LORD. When all the surrounding kingdoms heard that the LORD himself had fought against the enemies of Israel, the fear of God came over them. So Jehoshaphat's kingdom was at peace, for his God had given him rest on every side.[5]*

That's what we want: rest on every side. We want the joy of victory over the things that weigh us down. We want to come dancing back from our battles without being exhausted from all the fighting we did. We want to go through life and all its challenges not necessarily with comfort and ease but at least with a sense of freedom. And we know, according to God's Word, that we can.

I would love to hear God say in any given situation, "You don't have to fight this battle." And I believe that he does say that to us anytime we feel overwhelmed by our burdens. We may have to go out and take our positions and stand, but we don't have to do what only he can do. We don't have to arrange circumstances or manipulate people or worry about all the ways we can't do either of those things. We take our

> **We want to come dancing back from our battles without being exhausted from all the fighting we did. And according to God's Word, we can.**

positions, look to him, do only what he tells us to do, and leave the rest to him. That's the message of Scripture, and that's his desire.

God would not give us examples in Scripture like Jehoshaphat's battle if he didn't want us to apply them to ourselves. Jehoshaphat's victory-by-worship makes a great story, but it's more than entertaining history. Along with Peter's sleeping, Paul and Silas's prison worship, and David's psalms, it's a model that God wants us to learn from. His desire for his people is that we not be overwhelmed but live life fearlessly, faithfully, and freely. He wants us to fully depend on him and, like Jehoshaphat, have rest on every side.

Notes

INTRODUCTION

1. The word translated "fervently" or "earnestly" in Acts 12:5 (*ektenos*) is used very sparingly in the New Testament, and only twice in relation to prayer: here and in Luke 22:44, which describes the intensity of Jesus' prayers and his sweat being like drops of blood in the garden of Gethsemane.

CHAPTER 1: FREEDOM

1. Matthew 6:25
2. 1 Peter 5:7 (NIV), quoted from Psalm 55:22
3. Matthew 11:28
4. Psalm 55:22
5. Philippians 4:6
6. Hebrews 12:1
7. Isaiah 40:31
8. Galatians 6:2, NKJV
9. 2 Corinthians 11:28
10. Matthew 14:22-33
11. Even from the first words of Genesis, where the Spirit hovered over the dark and chaotic waters and had to tame them, the Jewish concept of the sea seemed to emphasize its mystery and turmoil. Hebrew Scripture speaks of "the deep" in terms of judgment (Noah's flood), an obstacle that God must overcome for his people and that he uses to overcome his enemies (the Red Sea), a chasm as dark as the grave (Job 38:16-17), and, when stirred up, a sign of God's disfavor (Jonah). Psalmists and prophets speak of the waters as a place of peril (Psalm 69:1, for example) and feel the need to remind us that God is present "even" there—as though there were

some question about that. The deep was not normally considered friendly territory. A necessary part of creation, perhaps, but always potentially wild and unpredictable.

CHAPTER 2: ROOTS

1. Matthew 25:14-30, NIV
2. Some parents take their "love" a lot further than that and actually do seek self-fulfillment and healing through their children. That's a problem and a certain path toward dysfunctional relationships. But even in perfectly healthy parent-child relationships, the parents will feel a certain weight of responsibility for the children and be burdened or stressed at times in their children's lives.
3. Matthew 6:25, 31, 34; 10:19; Mark 13:11; Luke 12:11, 22, 29
4. Romans 8:22
5. Ephesians 2:14, NIV
6. Romans 5:1; Philippians 4:7
7. Isaiah 9:6
8. 2 Corinthians 4:16
9. Romans 8:28
10. Peter Bourke, *A Better Way to Make a Living . . . and a Life: Thriving in the New World of Work* (Fairfax, VA: Xulon Press, 2009), 39–40.

CHAPTER 3: LOADS

1. "Overchoice," Wikipedia, http://en.wikipedia.org/wiki/Overchoice (accessed March 12, 2009).
2. Matthew 13:44-46
3. Proverbs 3:5-6
4. John 10:27
5. Proverbs 16:9
6. Exodus 31:13-17; Leviticus 23:3
7. Philippians 4:19
8. Exodus 15:26
9. Psalm 84:11; James 1:17
10. Proverbs 3:34; James 4:6; 1 Peter 5:5
11. Psalm 138:6; Proverbs 15:33; Isaiah 57:15; 66:2
12. John 11:3-6
13. Job 1:21
14. Genesis 50:20
15. John 8:36

CHAPTER 4: TRUST

1. Mark 4:38
2. Mark 4:40
3. Psalm 3:3, 5-6
4. The story is told in 2 Samuel 15–18.
5. Psalm 9:10
6. Psalm 22:5, NIV
7. Psalm 25:3
8. Psalm 34:10
9. Psalm 56:4, 11
10. Psalm 112:7
11. Psalm 125:1
12. Psalm 31:19
13. Psalm 32:10
14. Psalm 34:22
15. Psalm 50:15
16. Psalm 37:9
17. Psalm 37:3
18. Psalm 84:12
19. Psalm 63:11
20. Psalm 52:8
21. Psalm 37:5
22. Psalm 111:5
23. Psalm 115:9-11
24. Psalm 34:8
25. I address this more fully in the book *Fixing Abraham* (Carol Stream, IL: Tyndale House, 2009).
26. Mark 11:24, NIV
27. If you wonder whether this is true, compare how deflating the previous paragraph seems relative to how inspiring the description of trust's blessings was a few paragraphs earlier. I've found that the majority of people need to read or hear at least ten positive affirmations to balance out one negative word. At all costs, don't let this section on the difficulties in trusting God outweigh the greater truth of how trustworthy he is.
28. Hebrews 11:1, NKJV
29. 2 Corinthians 4:18
30. 2 Corinthians 5:7, NKJV
31. Psalm 36:8, NKJV
32. Romans 8:28
33. Jeremiah 29:11

34. There are numerous examples of this, including the crisis event that sent Joseph to Egypt; the plagues that made Israel's labor harder in Egypt—for a moment; the crisis of Goliath taunting Israel's armies; Daniel's mandatory dream interpretation; the threatened annihilation that prompted Esther to enter the king's court; and the Cross. In every case, God used a crisis as the stage for a reversal that further established or blessed his people.
35. Psalm 57:1
36. Proverbs 18:21
37. Mark 11:23
38. Romans 1:10; 1 Corinthians 16:5-7; 1 Thessalonians 3:11
39. Philippians 1:6
40. Philippians 1:18
41. Philippians 1:20
42. Job 2:9
43. Job 19:25-27, NIV
44. Romans 4:20
45. Hebrews 11:10
46. Genesis 15:1, NKJV
47. Genesis 22:14
48. Genesis 12:3

CHAPTER 5: RELEASE
1. Psalm 55:22; 1 Peter 5:7
2. Matthew 16:24
3. Galatians 2:20, NIV
4. Dr. and Mrs. Howard Taylor, *Hudson Taylor's Spiritual Secret* (Chicago: Moody Press, 1989), 162–163.
5. Hebrews 1:3, NIV
6. Philippians 2:3
7. Luke 6:38

CHAPTER 6: PASSION
1. Galatians 2:20
2. Romans 6:4
3. Hebrews 11:9-10
4. Colossians 3:1-4
5. 2 Corinthians 4:18
6. Matthew 13:44
7. *City Slickers*, Columbia Pictures, 1991.
8. Matthew 6:25-34

9. Matthew 6:33, NIV
10. Galatians 5:16
11. Philippians 1:27; 3:20
12. Philippians 2:1-11
13. Philippians 2:17
14. Philippians 3:8
15. Philippians 3:13
16. Philippians 4:4
17. Philippians 4:5
18. Philippians 4:6-7
19. Philippians 4:8
20. Philippians 4:11-12
21. Philippians 4:13
22. Philippians 4:19
23. Philippians 3:4-6
24. Philippians 3:7-9
25. Acts 6:1-6
26. This would be similar to a Korean or Russian church in the United States—an ethnic community worshiping in its own language in a foreign land. In the case of this synagogue, these would be Greek-speaking Jews living in Jerusalem, in many cases furthering their education under Temple-based rabbis. This fits Paul's profile perfectly.
27. 1 Thessalonians 5:18
28. Luke 14:26-27
29. John 4:34

CHAPTER 7: PERSPECTIVE
1. Louis C.K., interview by Conan O'Brien, *Late Night with Conan O'Brien*, NBC, October 1, 2008.
2. 1 Corinthians 15:19
3. Hebrews 11:10
4. Romans 4:20
5. 1 Corinthians 2:9
6. 2 Corinthians 4:17, NIV
7. Matthew 19:16-24
8. Luke 12:13-21
9. John 17:22-23
10. Ephesians 2:6
11. 1 Peter 2:9; Revelation 1:6
12. Revelation 3:21; 5:10; 22:5

13. Galatians 5:16
14. Romans 6:11
15. Galatians 6:2
16. Edward T. Welch, *When People Are Big and God Is Small: Overcoming Peer Pressure, Codependency, and the Fear of Man* (Phillipsburg, NJ: P&R Publishing, 1997).
17. See devotional for August 23 in Oswald Chambers, *Run This Race: The Complete Works of Oswald Chambers* (Grand Rapids, MI: Discovery House Publishers, 2000).
18. Revelation 1:17

CHAPTER 8: PRAISE
1. Acts 16:25
2. John 15:7
3. Numbers 22
4. Genesis 1:3—and almost identical wording in 1:6-7, 9, 11, 14-15, and 24
5. Proverbs 18:21
6. James 3:2, 5-10
7. Ephesians 4:29, NIV
8. Matthew 12:36
9. More information on Merlin Carothers and his books can be found at http://www.foundationofpraise.org.
10. Psalm 103:2
11. Acts 5:1-11
12. Psalm 16:11, NKJV
13. Isaiah 54:17
14. Ephesians 3:20
15. Psalm 103:1-2, italics added
16. Psalm 9:1-2, italics added
17. Psalm 34:1-3, italics added
18. Psalm 91:2, NIV
19. Psalm 42:5, 9-11, NIV
20. Psalm 4:8

CHAPTER 9: PRESENCE
1. Galatians 2:20, NIV
2. John 17:22-23
3. Ephesians 2:6
4. Ephesians 3:19, NIV
5. Philippians 2:13, NIV

6. Proverbs 3:5-6
7. Dr. and Mrs. Howard Taylor, *Hudson Taylor's Spiritual Secret* (Chicago: Moody Press, 1989), 157.

CONCLUSION
1. Judah's unfaithfulness would get much worse over the next couple of centuries, but even in Jehoshaphat's day there was widespread idolatry and shrines on hilltops throughout the country.
2. 2 Chronicles 20:12
3. 2 Chronicles 20:21
4. 2 Chronicles 20:22
5. 2 Chronicles 20:27-30

Made in United States
Orlando, FL
26 March 2022

16175178R00130